DORSET ILLUSTRATED

The County's Heritage in Prints and Drawings

Rocks near Bournemouth by Harry
Fenn showing lobster pots and a fishing
boat draped picturesquely with its nets.
This view, like the one of Corfe Castle
by T.L. Rowbotham on the previous
page, comes from *Picturesque Europe* of the
1880s. (Corfe Castle 165x150. Rocks near
Bournemouth 175x165).

DORSET ILLUSTRATED
The County's Heritage in Prints and Drawings

Alan W. Ball

Dorset Books

FOR MARION

First published in 2003 by Dorset Books
Copyright © 2003 Alan W. Ball

ISBN 1 871164 85 0

British Library Cataloguing-in-Publication-Data
A CIP data for this book is available from the British Library

DORSET BOOKS
Official Publisher to Dorset County Council

HALSGROVE
Halsgrove House
Lower Moor Way
Tiverton EX16 6SS
T: 01884 243242
F: 01884 243325
www.halsgrove.com

Printed and bound in Great Britain by
Bookcraft, Midsomer Norton

CONTENTS

A typically rural Dorset scene. It is a view
of Melbury Osmond by Edmund H. New
and comes from Bertram Windle's *Wessex
of Thomas Hardy* of 1902 (142 x 90).

GENERAL INTRODUCTION

Dorset is one of England's smaller counties, but has a wide variety of scenery from chalk uplands to watermeadows, valleys and the contrasting heathland stretching westwards from Wareham. The coastline is geologically one of the most interesting in the country with variations ranging from the Chesil Beach to Portland Bill, Lulworth Cove and Kimmeridge Bay. Fossils abound and the exceptional importance of the whole area has been recognised by its recent elevation to the status of a world heritage site.

Everywhere there are the remains of our earliest ancestors. Barrows, hill forts and great defensive earthworks are present in large numbers, though many sites have been damaged by nineteenth-century excavation and subsequent ploughing. The formidable ramparts of Maiden Castle are perhaps the most impressive remains followed by Hod Hill, Pilsdon Pen and Poundbury. Agriculture is still the predominant occupation and the county is made up almost entirely of villages and small towns with hardly any industry. Until the inclusion of Bournemouth after the 1974 boundary adjustments, there were few towns of any size other than Poole and except at this eastern edge it is an area with a markedly rural character.

Dorset has been singularly lucky in having a wide variety of building materials within its boundaries or close at hand. Outstanding of course is the availability of stone from the Portland quarries, which has been exported to the rest of the country for several centuries. In addition there is Purbeck marble, not a true marble, but a form of limestone. This has not only been used in church decoration, but also for roofing slates. When used for roofing they are so heavy they require a robust framework for support. Elsewhere in the county there were formerly locally worked limestone quarries and in the north a reliance on the warm Ham Hill stone from across the border in Somerset.

Spectacular buildings are not the style of Dorset and although parish churches are generally interesting with Perpendicular the predominant style, there are few of the stately towers, which are so marked a feature of neighbouring Somerset. There is no cathedral, as the see of the Bishop of Wessex was removed from Sherborne to Old Sarum as long ago as 1075. However Sherborne Abbey remains perhaps the most outstanding ecclesiastical building in the county and since the 1974 boundary alterations has been joined by Christchurch Priory. The two castles still with extensive remains are those at Corfe and Henry VIII's defensive fortification on Portland, built as part of a chain to defend the south coast against the French. This latter was put in hand almost immediately after Henry's return from the Field of the Cloth of Gold, at which he and the King of France had sworn undying friendship, an outstanding example of the trust placed by monarchs in each other's good intentions.

Fire seems to have been a particular hazard in the county. Apart from the coastal towns, which witnessed numerous conflagrations from the incursions of the French, Lyme Regis, Dorchester and especially Blandford all suffered through sheer carelessness. Blandford was almost completely gutted in 1731 and after its rebuilding at that date now presents one of the most perfect examples of eighteenth-century construction anywhere in the whole of England.

A number of travellers naturally visited Dorset over the years. In 1537 John Leland, one of the first English antiquaries, made a tour of the West Country. He found Lyme Regis 'A pretty market town set in the roots of a fine hill down to the hard shore' and passed through Weymouth, Lulworth and Poole on his way back to London. Celia Fiennes was an intrepid horsewoman and in 1698 made an extensive circuit of the north of England and back through the West Country. She was pleased with what she saw, but her robust non-conformist spirit was outraged at being refused admission by the owner of Forde Abbey. Daniel Defoe's *Tour Through the Whole Island of Great Britain* dates from 1724 to 1726. He found Dorset largely to his liking and felt Sherborne would have been a very pleasant place to which a person could retire and noted the high quality of the great number of sheep in the county.

Both Turner and Constable painted in Dorset, but it is not the object of the present book to deal with original works of art, but rather to provide a view of the county through the eyes of those who produced engravings, etchings and line drawings. The material that has survived from the past is uneven and that has naturally influenced what is presented here. I can only apologise in advance if some of your favourite illustrations do not appear, as there have been a large number from which to choose. As these illustrations often appear at a different size from the originals, I have included sizes in millimetres, with the height preceding the width. Rather than have a separate section on country houses, I have split them up throughout the book and grouped them with the nearest town. Finally it is recommended that the reader uses a magnifying glass to throw into sharper relief details in the illustrations that would otherwise escape the naked eye.

SHAFTESBURY AND GILLINGHAM

Shaftesbury is a town from which the tides of history have long since receded. It was founded by King Alfred in 880 and for his daughter he also created there the wealthiest Benedictine nunnery in the whole of England. The town stands on a commanding spur 700 feet above the surrounding countryside and in Gold Hill has one of the steepest streets in the kingdom. There were twelve medieval churches, only one of which survives, shrines, chantries, hospitals, four market crosses and a number of outstanding secular buildings that with the nunnery have all been swept away over the centuries.

Prosperity originally came to Shaftesbury because of the burial there in 980 of King Edward the Martyr, who was murdered at Corfe. It became a place of pilgrimage and miraculous cures and so until the Dissolution was a place of wealth and importance. Now it remains as a small country town.

The same is also true of Gillingham, which is a pleasant if unremarkable place and in the eighteenth century was engaged in the woollen trade. In the medieval period a royal forest stretched around it and provided a location of hunting and sport for kings and nobles.

Two seals of Shaftesbury from the first edition of John Hutchins' *History and Antiquities of the County of Dorset* published in 1774. The engraver is C. Hall (125 x 175).

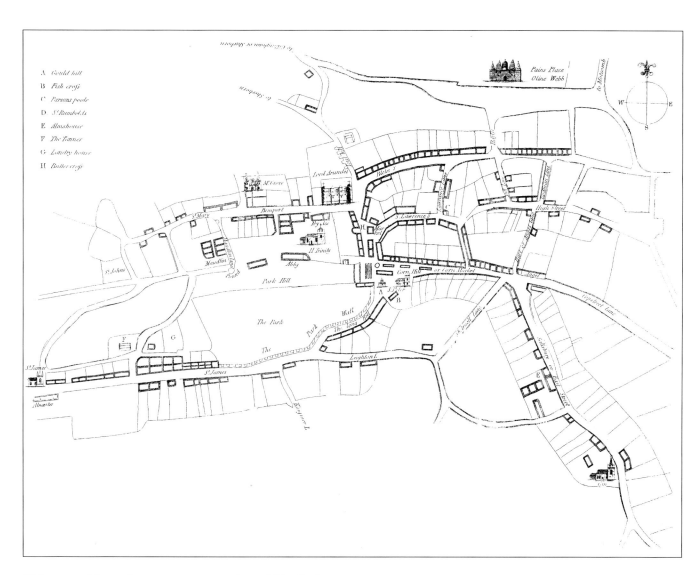

This reworking of an anonymous plan of Shaftesbury dated 1615 comes from the third edition of John Hutchins' *History and Antiquities of the County of Dorset* published between 1861 and 1873 and edited by W. Shipp and J.W. Hudson (220 x 295).

Two distant views of Shaftesbury. Above is an engraving dated 1 November 1804 by William Woolnoth after a drawing by George Shepherd from the *Beauties of England and Wales* (90 x 145) and below a sketch by Joseph Pennell from Sir Frederick Treves *Highways and Byways in Dorset* of 1906 (40 x 85).

Two further views of Shaftesbury by Joseph Pennell from Sir Frederick Treves' *Highways and Byways in Dorset*. Above is a group of old houses and below Gold Hill, which must be one of the steepest town streets in the whole country (above 45 x 90 and below 105 x 80).

The top of Gold Hill in Shaftesbury with the enormous-
ly buttressed wall on the left and a cobbled way for
pedestrians. This view by Edmund H. New comes from
Bertram Windle's *Wessex of Thomas Hardy* of 1902
(142 x 90).

A dwelling in the centre of Shaftesbury called Old Grove's House after a former owner. This is another of Edmund H. New's drawings from Bertram Windle's *Wessex of Thomas Hardy* (142 x 90).

People showing off their fashionable clothing as they walk around the church of St Mary the Virgin, Gillingham. The chancel is fourteenth century and the rest of the building dates from 1838 to 1839, except for the tower of 1908 by C.E. Ponting and some other twentieth-century additions by W.D. Caröe of 1921. The engraving is by Philip Brannon after one of his own drawings and it is included in the third edition of John Hutchins' *History and Antiquities of the County of Dorset* (85 x 155).

A view of Gillingham Mill by John Constable. The original oil painting probably of 1827 is in the Victoria and Albert Museum and this engraving by David Lucas dates from 1845 eight years after Constable's death (180 x 150).

The church of Saints George and Gregory, Marnhull, which is largely Perpendicular and Victorian in construction. The artist is Philip Brannon and this view comes from the third edition of John Hutchins' *History and Antiquities of the County of Dorset* (100 x 155).

In the foreground the great or Wyndham's oak at Silton near Gillingham as it was in the early nineteenth century. Already at that date it was a tree of great age and hollow inside. In the background stands the late Norman church of St Nicholas containing an excellent fan vault in the north chapel. In addition there is an elaborate monument of 1692 by John Nost showing the standing figure of Sir Hugh Wyndham, a Justice of the Court of Common Pleas. Wyndham used to love to sit under the oak to smoke a pipe and contemplate 'the rich, cheerful and extensive prospect its site commands'. The engraving is by John Greig after a drawing by J. Fenton and comes from the *Antiquarian and Topographical Cabinet* of 1817 to 1819 (60 x 85).

BLANDFORD FORUM

Blandford is a small town on the River Stour between Salisbury and Dorchester and it possess one of the best groupings of Georgian buildings in England. This is not the result of chance development, but rather because of the rebuilding after a disastrous fire in 1731, which started in a tallow chandler's house and proved as devastating for Blandford as the Great Fire was for London. Interestingly it also had the effect of halting an epidemic of smallpox in its tracks, much as at London the plague of 1665 was cleansed by the conflagration in the City the following year.

In the eighteenth century Defoe noted that Blandford was famous for its lace making, 'As I think I never saw a better in Flanders, France or Italy' and it was lucky that after the fire William and John Bastard were the surveyors in charge of the rebuilding work and gave the town the character it still largely retains.

The bridge over the River Stour in Blandford. The sketch by Charles G. Harper comes from his book the *Exeter Road* of 1899 (95 x 130).

Two almost exactly similar views of the centre of Blandford. Above is the version by Joseph Pennell from Sir Frederick Treves' *Highways and Byways in Dorset* of 1906 (65 x 90) and below that of Charles G. Harper also from his book the *Exeter Road* (95 x 150).

An anonymous line drawing of Blandford's old church destroyed in the great conflagration of 1731, which devastated nearly the whole of the town centre. It comes from the third edition of John Hutchins' *History and Antiquities of the County of Dorset* (320 x 185).

N

A

W

E

B

S

A. *Chapel of the Ryves family.*
B. *Chapel of the Rogers family.*

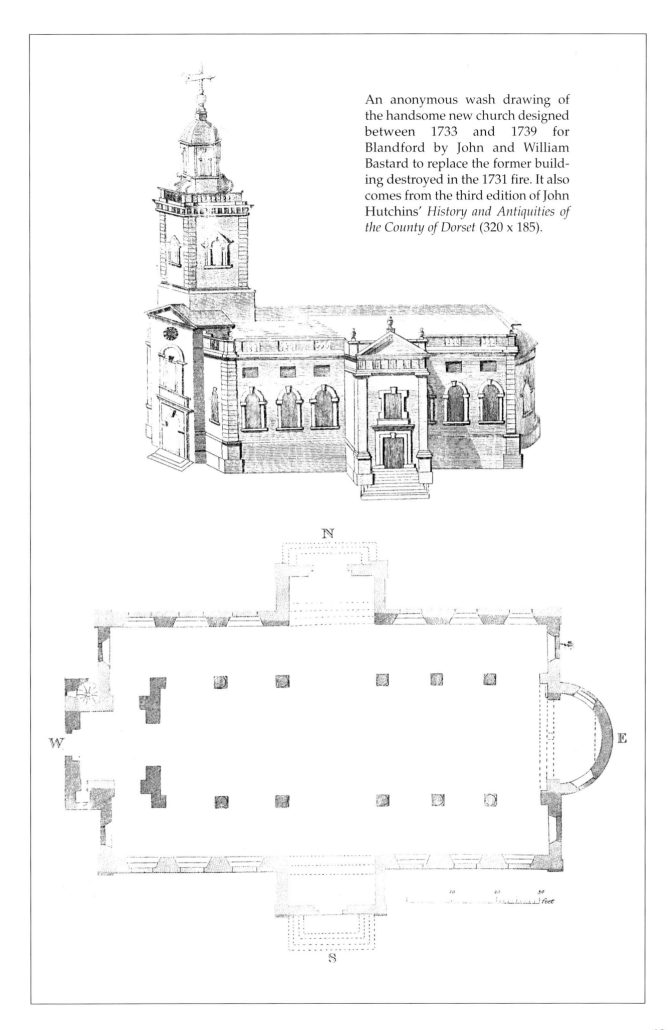

An anonymous wash drawing of the handsome new church designed between 1733 and 1739 for Blandford by John and William Bastard to replace the former building destroyed in the 1731 fire. It also comes from the third edition of John Hutchins' *History and Antiquities of the County of Dorset* (320 x 185).

19

Almshouses at
Milton, Dorset
Sidney Heath

Between 1771 and 1790 the powerful local landowner, the Earl of Dorchester, swept away the former small town of Milton Abbey and these almshouses of about 1674, originally in the old settlement, were moved and re-erected on their present site in 1779. The view is by Sidney Heath and comes from his *Old English Houses of Alms* of 1910 (200 x 165).

After the Dissolution the monastic buildings of Milton Abbey except for the enormous church were converted into the mansion of Sir John Tregonwell. From 1769 onwards the Earl of Dorchester employed Sir William Chambers to tear down all but the abbot's hall and construct a new mansion. Joseph Nash in his *Mansions of England in the Olden Time* published between 1838 to 1849 depicts buildings in their original state, complete with furniture, fittings and people dressed appropriately for the period. This view of Sir John Tregonwell's house shows one of Nash's imaginative reconstructions (140 x 195).

The former monastic church at Milton Abbey, which became parochial at the Dissolution. It is extremely large, measuring 136 feet in length and this view by Joseph Pennell comes from Sir Frederick Treves' *Highways and Byways in Dorset* of 1906 (52 x 90). Below is the house at Milton Abbey which after 1954 became a school. This representation of the building designed by Sir William Chambers between 1771 and 1774 for the Earl of Dorchester comes from Jones' *Views of the Seats of Noblemen and Gentlemen* of 1829. It is an engraving by William Radclyffe after a drawing by J.P. Neale (85 x 130).

Cattle graze and trees are reflected in the water by the rustic bridge looking across to Bryanston, the simple house demolished in 1890 to make way for Lord Portman's grand building designed for him by Richard Norman Shaw between 1890 and 1894. This later became Bryanston School in 1927. This engraving by V.W. Picot after a drawing by W. Tomkins comes from the first edition of John Hutchins' *History and Antiquities of the County of Dorset* of 1774 (200 x 400).

Another view of the original Bryanston engraved by J. Emes after a drawing by J. Laport and dated 1 June 1794, which is included in the third edition of John Hutchins' *History and Antiquities of the County of Dorset* (180 x 300).

Two views of Whatcombe House which was built in 1750 and enlarged in 1802. The distant view with a large number of cattle is an engraving dated 25 November 1814 by J. Landseer from a drawing by Richard Kerby (185 x 295) and the near view with sheep and a shepherd is an engraving by J.H. Le Keux from his own drawing (150 x 185). Both views also come from the third edition of John Hutchins' *History and Antiquities of the County of Dorset*.

Langton House of 1827 to 1833 by C.R. Cockerell was demolished in 1949 and because of the construction date this undated engraving must be by the youngest of the three James Basires, father, son and grandson, all of whom were engravers. The view shows the house embowered in trees with people admiring the landscape and it is included in the third edition of John Hutchins' *History and Antiquities of the County of Dorset* (195 x 305).

The original Crichel House was destroyed by fire in 1742 and rebuilding started in the following year. Enlargement took place in 1765 and there were alterations in 1869 and again in 1950. The interior has some highly attractive seventeenth century rooms, partially in the style of Kent and later in that of Wyatt. This anonymous engraving also comes from the third edition of John Hutchins' *History and Antiquities of the County of Dorset* (195 x 235).

Two views of houses drawn and engraved by Philip Brannon for the third edition of John Hutchins' *History and Antiquities of the County of Dorset*. Above is Blandford St Mary Manor House, which consists of two seventeenth-century ranges at right angles to each other (60 x 90) and below Winterbourne Clenston House that is Tudor with seventeenth-century extensions built in warm Ham Hill stone (145 x 250).

Two views of churches drawn and engraved by Philip Brannon for the third edition of John Hutchins' *History and Antiquities of the County of Dorset*. Above is St. Nicholas, Durweston with a Perpendicular tower and the remainder by P.C. Hardwick of 1847 (85 x 155) and below Holy Cross, Shillington, with groups of people by the entrance porch. The building has a Perpendicular tower with a Norman nave and chancel and a north aisle and north arcade of 1888 by F.W. Hunt (100 x 155).

WIMBORNE MINSTER

efoe writes about Wimborne Minster in the following unflattering terms: 'There I found nothing remarkable but the church, which is indeed a very great one, ancient, and yet very well built with a very firm, strong tower, considerably high: but was without doubt much finer when on top of it stood a most exquisite spire, finer and taller if fame lies not, than that at Salisbury and by its situation in a plainer, flatter country, visible no question much farther: but this most beautiful ornament was blown down by a sudden tempest of wind, as they tell us, in the year 1622'. As Salisbury possesses the tallest spire of any cathedral in England this claim seems highly dubious.

The Minster has in fact two towers, and still however remains a noble and imposing edifice. The rest of the town is unremarkable, but sits comfortably within boundaries, which have not been encroached upon by a mass of modern development.

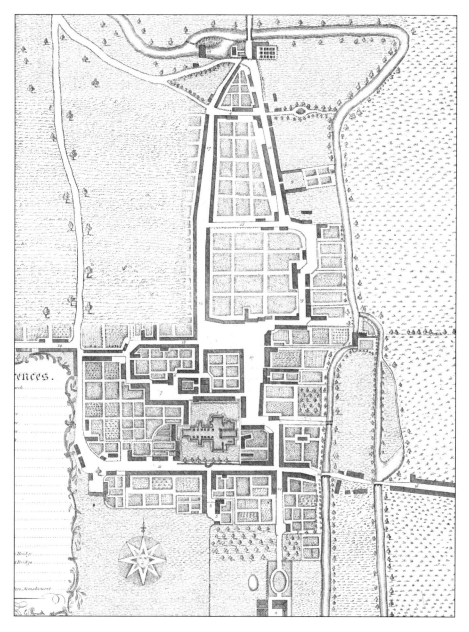

An anonymous and undated plan of Wimborne Minster
from the third edition of John Hutchins' *History and
Antiquities of the County of Dorset* (310 x 265).

Two distant views of Wimborne Minster in high
summer by Joseph Pennell from Sir Frederick Treves'
Highways and Byways in Dorset of 1906 (Above 40 x 90
and below 55 x 90).

The actual minster in Wimborne Minster. A nunnery was founded in the town in 705, which was destroyed by the Danes in the late tenth-century. Edward the Confessor then created a college of secular canons that was dissolved in 1537 at the Dissolution. No collegiate buildings survive except for the church. The nave, crossing tower and transepts are Norman, but the building had restoration by T.H. Wyatt in 1857 and J.L. Pearson in 1891. The west tower was built between 1448 and 1464 and it has been said that being almost the same height as the crossing tower produces an uneasy relationship between the two. The crossing tower had a spire until blown down in 1600 (not 1622 as Defoe stated) and this would have created a feeling of dominance until that date. Perhaps the whole building should be called imposing rather than elegant. Above is an engraving dated 1 February 1803 by J. Smith from a drawing by T. Nash in the *Beauties of England and Wales* (90 x 150) and below an engraving from the north west by J. Fisher from a drawing by W. Waller, which appears in Peter Hall's *Historical and Descriptive Guide to the Town of Wimborne Minster* of 1830 (100 x 150).

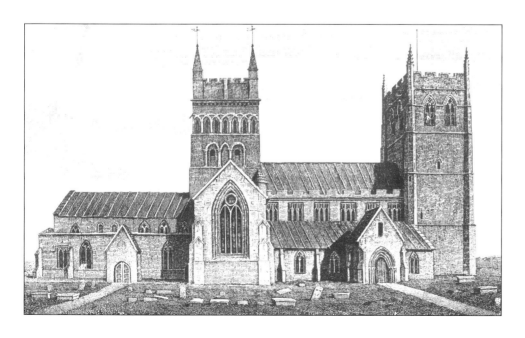

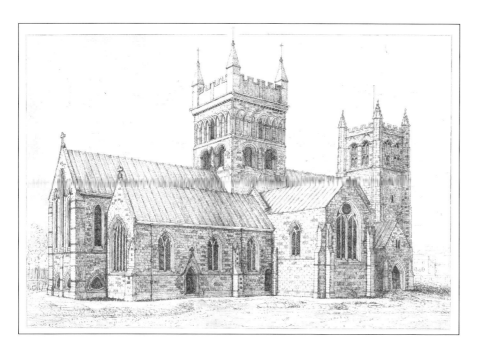

Two further views of the minster in Wimborne Minster. The one above from the north east is included in Charles Mayo's *History of Wimborne Minster* of 1861 with no indication of the artist (110 x 160) and that below from the north west is by Joseph Pennell and comes from Sir Frederick Treves' *Highways and Byways in Dorset* of 1906 (65 x 90).

Two depictions of the crossing tower of Wimborne Minster. Above is an anonymous elevation and section of the central tower and transepts included in Charles Mayo's *History of Wimborne Minster* of 1860 (130 x 85) and below an anonymous drawing from the third edition of John Hutchins' *History and Antiquities of the County of Dorset* (130 x 80).

The monument to the Duke and Duchess of Somerset in Wimborne Minster. The artist responsible for this view is one of the two Schnebbelies, Jacob or his son Robert and the engraver one of the three James Basires, father, son or grandson. This all makes the dating of the engraving somewhat problematical. It comes from the third edition of John Hutchins' *History and Antiquities of the County of Dorset* (385 x 255).

A further engraving showing a great deal of detail of the Duke and Duchess of Somerset's monument in Wimborne Minster. The engraving is by Henry Le Keux after a drawing by Edward Blore from his *Monumental Remains of Noble and Eminent Persons* of 1826 (210 x 130).

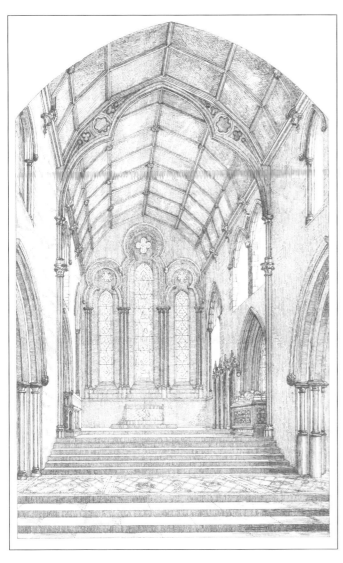

Above is an anonymous engraving of the presbytery of Wimborne Minster from Charles Mayo's *History of Wimborne Minster* of 1860 (170 x 110) and below a view of the former leper hospital and now almshouses in Pamphill, just outside and to the north west of Wimborne. The building seems to be early thirteenth century in origin and was renovated at the beginning of the twentieth century. The illustration is by Sidney Heath from his *Old English Houses of Alms* of 1910 (145 x 115).

St Giles in Wimborne St Giles is a house originally of 1672 with considerable additions by Henry Flitcroft from 1740 to 1744. There were further alterations in 1790 and 1813 and finally important changes by P.C. Hardwick in 1854. The interiors are largely the work of Flitcroft and this anonymous view comes from *Historic Houses of the United Kingdom* of 1892 with the text on St Giles by Mary Francis Billington (135 x195).

Kingston Lacy

Kingston Lacy is owned by the National Trust and is one of the most important surviving houses by Sir Roger Pratt. It is a fine example of a Carolean building even allowing for Sir Charles Barry's alterations of 1835 to 1836. It was built originally from 1663 to 1665 for Sir Ralph Bankes in contrast to the no longer habitable Corfe Castle, the home of his father Sir John. This drawing is by Sidney Heath from his book *Some Dorset Manor Houses* written in conjunction with W. de C. Prideaux in 1907 (175 x 230).

Cranborne Manor House started life in 1207 as a medieval hunting lodge, which was remodelled in the reign of James 1 from 1608 to 1611. There were additions in 1640 and alterations in 1647 with the interiors now being mainly nineteenth century. These two views by William Curtis Green are from the *Builder* of 5 August 1899 (above 130 x 150 and below 125 x 160).

Cranborne Manor House as seen by Joseph
Nash from his *Mansions of England in the
Olden Time* of 1838 to 1849. In this view Nash
creates the atmosphere and dress of the house
in the seventeenth century (205 x 140).

Charborough House was built prior to 1661 with extensions in the eighteenth century and alterations by John Nash in 1810 including a new roof. The south-west turret dates from 1840 and this view comes from *Some Dorset Manor Houses* of 1907 by Sidney Heath and W. de C. Prideaux, with the artist being Heath himself (220 x 182).

Canford Manor

Sidney Heath

At Canford

Another of Sidney Heath's drawings from *Some Dorset Manor Houses*. It is of Canford Manor with a fifteenth-century kitchen and the remainder several shades of Victorian. From 1825 to 1836 Edward Blore rebuilt the former house, then came what amounted to an almost total rebuild again by Sir Charles Barry after 1847 with further remodelling and additions in 1851, 1873 to 1876 and in 1888. The building now houses Canford School (200 x 170).

Two illustrations from the third edition of John Hutchins' *History and Antiquities of the County of Dorset*. Above is an engraving by Thomas Bonnor of Merly House near Canford Magna built between 1752 and 1760 (195 x 360) and below an engraving by one of the three James Basires of Gaunt's House in Hinton Martell, which is now a school. It is a large building of 1886 to 1887, which encases an 1809 five-bay villa by William Evans, who made the undated drawing on which the Basire engraving is based (180 x 350).

BOURNEMOUTH AND CHRISTCHURCH

oth Bournemouth and Christchurch are Johnnies come lately as far as Dorset is concerned, as they have only been part of the geographical county since the boundary adjustments of 1974. However, Bournemouth is now the largest town in Dorset and one of England's premier seaside resorts. The story begins in 1810 when when Louis Tregonwell built himself a house in the area, but it was really Sir George Tapps-Gervis, who commissioned Benjamin Ferrey in 1836 to design the Westover Estate that started the march of villadom through chine and pine. To this day Bournemouth remains a green and pleasant land with plenty of open space, although sadly very little of the original Westover Estate remains. Bournemouth like most English seaside towns has had to change to meet the challenge of cheap package holidays abroad and is now a very different place from its heyday in the inter-war period.

Christchurch by contrast is small and quiet and clustered round the great Augustinian priory church founded in 1150, but with an important church on the site long before that. The scant remains of a medieval castle survive and there are one or two pleasant eighteenth-century buildings to complete the picture.

Adelaide Cottages and Rustic Bridge in Bournemouth with pine trees much in evidence. The view is an engraving by Philip Brannon after one of his own drawings included in his *Illustrated Historical and Picturesque Guide to Bournemouth* published in the 1850s (110 x 165).

The seashore of Bournemouth with fishing boats much in evidence from an engraving dated 1 July 1855 by Philip Brannon after one of his own drawings. It comes from his *Illustrated Historical and Picturesque Guide to Bournemouth* (180 x 175).

Two further views by Philip Brannon from his *Illustrated Historical and Picturesque Guide to Bournemouth*. Above is an engraving dated 1 July 1855 showing the Belle Vue Hotel and Reading Room with a simple pier, bathing machines and people looking out to sea (100 x 145). Below an undated but obviously later engraving showing a much enlarged pier with people waiting for the paddle steamer and villas marching up the pine clad hills (115 x 180).

Sir George Tapps-Gervis commissioned Benjamin Ferrey in 1836 to design the Westover Estate with select villas, most of which had vanished by 1930. Both of these engravings by Philip Brannon after his own drawings are dated 1 July 1855 and come from his *Illustrated Historical and Picturesque Guide to Bournemouth*. Above is the Bath Hotel in Westover Road and below a house called Portman Lodge (both 70 x 115).

Similar buildings to those on the previous page, also dated 1 July 1855 and engraved by Philip Brannon after his own drawings in the *Illustrated Historical and Picturesque Guide to Bournemouth*. Above is Alma House, Alma Road and below 'the offices of Mr Rebbeck, House Agent' in Gervis Place (both 70 x 100).

Two further buildings represented by Philip Brannon's engravings after his own drawings in the *Illustrated Historical and Picturesque Guide to Bournemouth*. Above is the Sanitorium for Consumptive Diseases of the Chest in Alumhurst Road (now a convalescent home) which was built in 1855 to the designs of E.B. Lamb (85 x 120). Below is St Peter's church in Bournemouth, which was built in sections over a period of almost forty years. The original part was constructed from 1841 to 1843 by John Tulloch of Wimborne, a south aisle was added by Edmund Pearce in 1851, G.E. Street built on a nave and north aisle from 1854 to 1859 and an east end followed from 1860 to 1864. Finally a tower was begun in 1869 and finished by a spire in 1879 (90 x 120).

This engraving by T. Heaviside after a drawing by B. Sly shows how Street was planning the completion of St Peter's, which was only achieved nearly a decade after this view in the *Builder* of 24 December 1870 (275 x 170).

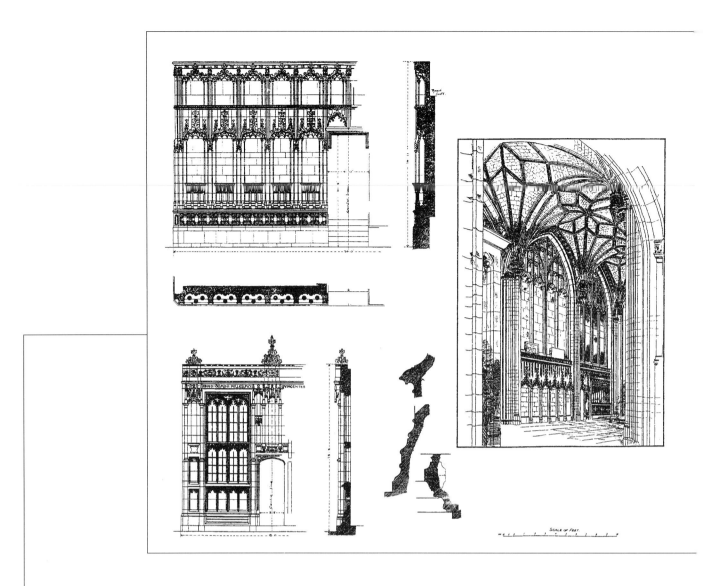

Below is the north elevation of Christchurch Priory and above details of the interior. The foundation became an Augustinian priory in 1150, but was already important at the time of the Domesday survey. There is Norman and a great deal of Early English work with a restoration in 1862 by Benjamin Ferrey, whose father was mayor of Christchurch. Both the elevation and details are by E. Bernard Hutchinson and come from the *Builder* of 25 July 1891 (elevation 160 x 380 and details 265 x 385).

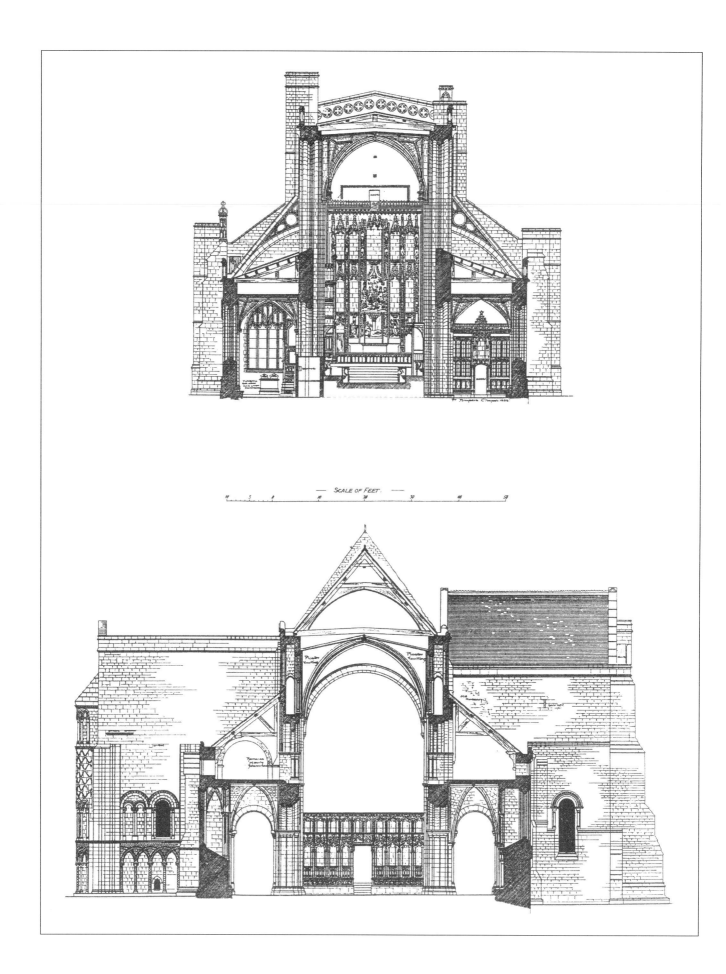

SCALE OF FEET.

Above is a cross section through the choir of Christchurch Priory and below
one through the nave. Both are also by E. Bernard Hutchinson from the
Builder of 25 July 1891 (choir 95 x 115 and nave 115 x 180).

Two views of Christchurch Priory. Above is an engraving by Edward Finden after a drawing by William Westall from *Great Britain Illustrated* of 1830 with a text by Thomas Moule, better known for his cartographic work (92 x 145). Below is an engraving by James Storer after his own drawing of 1811 published in *Ancient Reliques* of the following year. It shows the eastern end of the priory with three figures in conversation (70 x 100).

The impressive chantry in Christchurch Priory to Margaret, Countess of Salisbury, who was beheaded in 1541. The engraving is by John le Keux after a drawing by Edward Blore in his *Monumental Remains of Noble and Eminent Persons* of 1826 (200 x 140).

POOLE

Poole was founded in about 1180 to take advantage of the great harbour, as the River Frome at Wareham started to silt up and become less and less able to take reasonably sized ships. Poole had a borough charter by 1248 and was a staple port by 1433. Its great period of prosperity was in the eighteenth century when the Newfoundland fishing trade was at its height. However much of this prosperity also depended on the lucrative side lines of piracy, smuggling and creating general mayhem on the high seas.

One of the most notorious Poole buccaneers was Harry Page, who was known to the French as Arripay. On one occasion he returned home with no less than a hundred and twenty prizes picked up off the coast of Brittany and it was therefore no surprise that the French should attack Poole and try to smoke him out of his lair. Page and his followers put up stout resistance, but when matters became too hot they fled prudently to the great heath that stretches from Wareham almost to Dorchester.

In the nineteenth century Poole gradually lost its influence to the rising prosperity of Bournemouth and in the post Second World War period the heart of the town was treated shabbily by developers. Respectability descended on Poole and the stirring days of Arripay now seem a very long time ago.

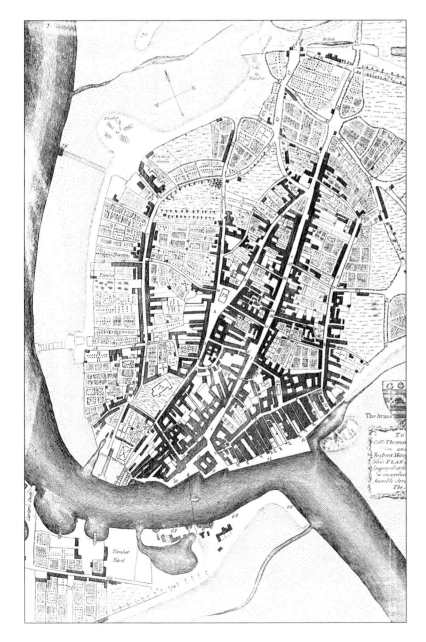

An anonymous and undated map of Poole from the first edition of John Hutchins' *History and Antiquities of the County of Dorset* of 1774 (340 x 230).

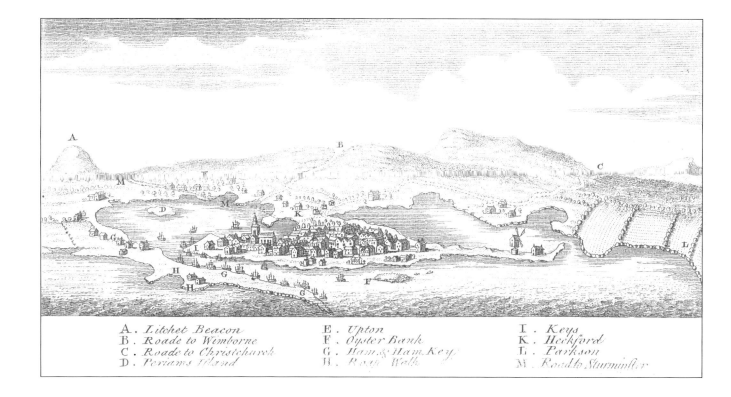

A . Litchet Beacon
B . Roade to Wimborne
C . Roade to Christchurch
D . Periams Island
E . Upton
F . Oyster Bank
G . Ham & Ham Key
H . Ropp Walk
I . Keys
K . Heckford
L . Parkson
M . Roade to Sturminster

Above is a view entitled a *Prospect of the Town of Poole From the West End of Brunksea (Brownsea) Island*, which must be prior to 1770 the date at which the artist John Bastard died. The engraver is James Mynde and the prospect comes from the third edition of John Hutchins' *History and Antiquities of the County of Dorset* (80 x 175). Below is a glimpse of Poole estuary by Joseph Pennell from Sir Frederick Treves' *Highways and Byways in Dorset* of 1906 (65 x 90).

Above is an anonymous view of Poole harbour from the *Rivers of Great Britain – South and West Coasts* of 1897 (105 x 128) and below a drawing of the harbour by Joseph Pennell from Sir Frederick Treves' *Highways and Byways in Dorset* (65 x 90).

Two further drawings of Poole by Joseph Pennell from Sir Frederick Treves' *Highways and Byways in Dorset* of 1906. Above is a view of the harbour (55 x 85) and below is a sketch of the Quay (65 x 90).

Above is another of Joseph Pennell's drawings of the quay at Poole from Sir Frederick Treves' *Highways and Byways in Dorset*. It shows the Harbour Office and so-called Town Cellar (60 x 85). The view below is of the Guildhall built in 1761, which is by Charles Harper from his book the *Dorset Coast* of 1905 (95 x 135).

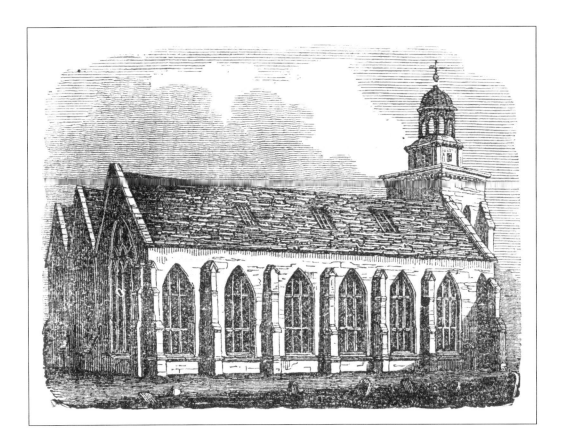

The two churches of St James in Poole. Above is an engraving of the medieval church demolished in 1819 (65 x 90) and below its solid and roomy replacement of the following year by the architects John Kent of Southampton and Joseph Hannaford of Christchurch (125 x 175). Both views come from John Sydenham's *History of Poole* of 1839.

Above is a modest little anonymous engraving of the modest little New Inn in Poole as it existed in the 1830s. Below is a view by Nathaniel Whittock of St Paul's church, a pleasant Grecian building erected in 1833 'at the upper end of the High Street to meet the religious wants of the increasing population of the town'. It was demolished in 1963. Both views also come from John Sydenham's *History of Poole* (above 65 x 90 and below 120 x 180).

Two trade advertisements engraved by Philip Brannon
after his own drawings from his *Illustrated Historical and
Picturesque Guide to Bournemouth*. Both are dated 1 July
1855 and show two business premises in Poole. Above
is the Antelope Hotel (75 x 110) and below Brine
Brothers, Tea Dealers (75 x 115).

Two engravings from John Sydenham's *History of Poole* of 1839. Above is a view of St George's almshouses in Church Street, founded before 1429, but altered after that date (40 x 90). Below is the original St Peter's church designed in 1833 to 1834 by John Tulloch of Wimborne. The artist is Nathaniel Whittock. A replacement for Tulloch's building was constructed piecemeal from 1876 to 1901 by Frederick Rogers, J.L. and F.L. Pearson (110 x 175).

A view of Brownsea Island by C.G. Harper from his
Dorset Coast of 1905 (50 x 90).

A sketch of Poole Harbour and its islands including part
of Brownsea Island. It is by Douglas Snowdon and
comes from the *Book of Bournemouth,* a publication created for a meeting of the British Medical Association held
there in July 1934 (110 x 170).

Above is a crude engraving of a south-east view of Brownsea Island and Castle with a river that seems to end in mid-air and looks peculiarly like a large snake. It comes from the 1774 edition of John Hutchins' *History and Antiquities of the County of Dorset* (80 x 175).

Above is a north-east view of the island and Castle from the third edition of the same publication. The engraver is Thomas Vivaries and the artist somebody simply called Bretherton (300 x 450).

Two views of Brownsea Castle after 1852 alterations, which turned it into a castellated country house. Both are by Philip Brannon and appear in the *Companion to Hutchins' History: The Coast Scenery of Dorset* published by R. Sydenham at Poole in 1862 (both 130 x 190).

WAREHAM

Wareham today is a small peaceful town sitting within large earthen ramparts and a coastal frontage that has a leisurely air. Its former trading capacity was lost to Poole with the silting up of its river and today's peace is in marked contrast to an extremely bloody past. The earthen ramparts go back beyond the Romans and were regularly tested when the Danes and Saxons were at each other's throats, again during the insurgency of Stephen's reign and especially during the Civil War. In between these major upheavals were numerous alarums, attacks, sackings, burnings and general disorder. There was also for good measure a disastrous fire in 1762 and hardly anything survives prior to that date. At one time there was a castle, but its position is only marked by the scantiest of remains. All in all it is something of a miracle that Wareham has survived into its present placid old age.

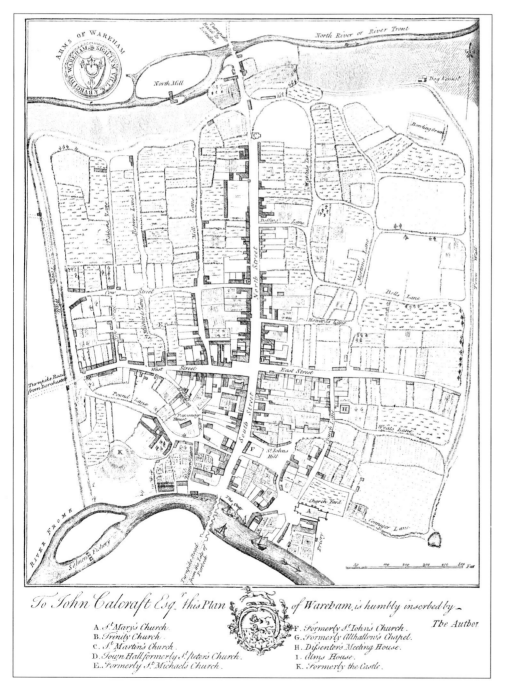

An anonymous and undated plan of Wareham included in the first edition of John Hutchins' *History and Antiquities of the County of Dorset* of 1774. It shows the Congregational church in Church Lane of 1762 as Dissenters' Meeting House, so the plan must be after that date (275 x 225).

Two views of Wareham by Joseph Pennell from Sir Frederick Treves' *Highways and Byways in Dorset* of 1906. Above is the approach to Wareham by the north causeway (55 x 90) and below the Quay (50 x 90).

St Martin's church in Wareham has some Saxon work and in about 1200 a north aisle was added. The tower appears to be sixteenth century and there has been a certain amount of repair work to other parts of the fabric. Above is an engraving by somebody simply called Pearson after a drawing by J.J. Hissey from his book *On Southern Roads* of 1896 (100 x 165) and below another of Joseph Pennell's sketches from Sir Frederick Treves' *Highways and Byways in Dorset* (85 x 90).

Two views of Wareham by Edmund H. New from Bertram Windle's *Wessex of Thomas Hardy* of 1902 (above 142 x 90 and below 70 x 80).

A crude engraving by somebody simply called Bayly of a
north view of St Mary's church in Wareham with a large
number of tombs in the graveyard looking curiously like gift
boxes. It comes from the first edition of John Hutchins' *History
and Antiquities of the County of Dorset* of 1774 (240 x 200).

Above is a distant view of Wareham with Corfe Castle in the far background. It is by
E.H. New and comes from Bertram Windle's *Wessex of Thomas Hardy* of 1902 (45 x 60).
Below is a view of Wool Manor House, which dates from the seventeenth century. The
drawing is by Sidney Heath from his book *Some Dorset Manor Houses* written in 1907
in conjunction with W. de C. Prideaux (85 x 148).

Wool Manor House

Wool
Manor
House

Sidney Heath

The
Kitchen

Further views of Wool Manor House by Sidney Heath from
the same source as the work on the previous page (whole
page 225 x 175).

The "Philip and Joanna" Bowl
at Bloxworth House

Gardener's Cottage
dated 1560.

Dated Stone
on Stables

Bloxworth House

Bloxworth House is north west of Wareham and the original part dates from 1608 to which have been added a number of later alterations. These views by Sidney Heath come from the source as those on the previous two pages (whole page 200 x 175).

Mapperton House north east of Bridport is mainly sixteenth and seventeenth century in construction. Above is a drawing of the house by William Curtis Green from the *Builder* of 20 August 1904 (120 x 180) and below another of Sidney Heath's views from *Some Dorset Manor Houses* (160 x 270).

Mapperton Manor House

Two illustrations of country houses from the third edition of John
Hutchins' *History and Antiquities of the County of Dorset*. Above is the
sixteenth-century Tyneham House, the east front of which was taken
down by the Ministry of Works in 1967 and the porch moved to Bingham's
Melcombe (see pages 158, 175 and 176). The engraving is by J.H. Le Keux
after his own drawing (145 x 270). Below is another engraving by J.H. Le
Keux after his own drawing. It is of Creech Grange, which still retains
sixteenth-century elements, although the house is now mainly eighteenth
and nineteenth century (150 x 285).

Thomson Manor House in Winterborne Thomson (or now more usually Tomson) appears to date from the late-sixteenth or early-seventeenth century. The engraving above by Philip Brannon from his own drawing shows three well-dressed visitors approaching the entrance embowered in summer foliage. The view comes also from the third edition of John Hutchins' work (130 x 190). Below is a south-east view of Bindon Abbey very little of which now remains. It was founded as a Cistercian house in 1149 and transferred to Bindon itself in 1172. The engraver is the oldest of the James Basires and maybe the artist is the person depicted as sketching in the foreground, although whether he is drawing the ruins or the goats is hard to determine. The view comes from the first edition of John Hutchins' work of 1774 (155 x 210).

Two views in Bere Regis drawn and engraved by Philip Brannon for the third edition of John Hutchin's *History and Antiquities of the County of Dorset*. Above is a representation of the church of St John the Baptist, which has a long and interesting history. There is possible Anglo-Saxon work at the north-east corner of the nave followed by twelfth and thirteenth century construction in the main body of the building. In addition there is a substantial Perpendicular tower (155 x 195). Below is a view of Bere Regis House which sadly today is only represented by trivial remains in a field to the east of the church (60 x 90).

SWANAGE AND CORFE

Swanage is an attractive seaside town overtaken by 'delusions of metropolitan grandeur'. This is due to a London building and construction contractor, George Burt, who hailed originally from Swanage and was determined to bestow forgotten trifles, and sometimes a lot more than trifles, from his contractor's yard on his native town. He donated a town hall in 1872 and eleven years later enlivened its facade with that of the seventeenth-century Mercers' Hall, which had just been demolished. This was in fact a splendid mixture of panels carved with fruit, volutes, an open segmental pediment and flying putti in relief holding a bust of Flora, the Mercers' emblem. The other bits and pieces include a clock tower of 1854, originally set up on the south side of London Bridge as a memorial to the Iron Duke, ionic columns, lamp standards bearing the names of central London parishes and in 1890 a cliff top café in the shape of a castle.

After this one can retire thankfully to the attractive village of Corfe where there is of course a genuine medieval castle, now looking decidedly the worse for wear as it was slighted in 1645 after capture by the Parliamentary forces in the Civil War.

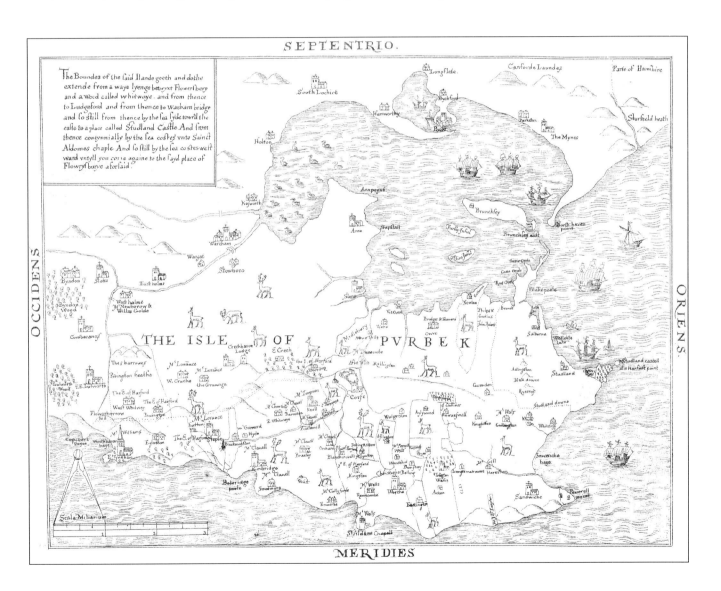

Ralph Treswell the elder is the cartographer responsible for this map of the Isle of Purbeck of about 1585. He is perhaps best known for his famous pictorial pre-Great Fire maps of London and this pictorial approach can be seen clearly in the facsimile included in the third edition of John Hutchins' *History and Antiquities of the County of Dorset* (200 x 255).

Two sketches of Swanage. Above is a view by Edmund H. New from Bertram Windle's *Wessex of Thomas Hardy* of 1902 (50 x 90) and below a drawing by Joseph Pennell from Sir Frederick Treves' *Highways and Byways in Dorset* of 1906 (65 x 85).

Two drawings of Swanage by Charles G. Harper from his *Dorset Coast* of 1905. Above is a sketch of the High Street and Town Hall (100 x 140) and below the Wellington Memorial, which had stood originally on the south side of London Bridge and was donated to the town by the contractor George Burt (100 x 155).

The road to Studland and a view in Studland itself. Both drawings are by Joseph Pennell from Sir Frederick Treves' *Highways and Byways in Dorset* of 1906 (Above 65 x 85 and below 65 x 90).

Two sketches of the coastline by Charles G. Harper from his *Dorset Coast* of 1905. Above is Parsons Barn, which somehow recalls the old smuggling phrase of 'brandy for the parson and baccy for the clerk', while below are the highly distinctive cliffs of St Aldhelm's Head (above 120 x 85 and below 95 x 165).

Above is an anonymous engraving of Smedmore House, which has a romantic setting close to the sea a mile south east of Kimmeridge. The building is mentioned as early as 1632, but it is predominantly eighteenth century in construction. The engraving is dated 10 July 1840 and comes from the third edition of John Hutchins' *History and Antiquities of the County of Dorset* (200 x 300). Below is a sketch of Worbarrow Bay by Charles G. Harper from his *Dorset Coast* of 1905 (45 x 80).

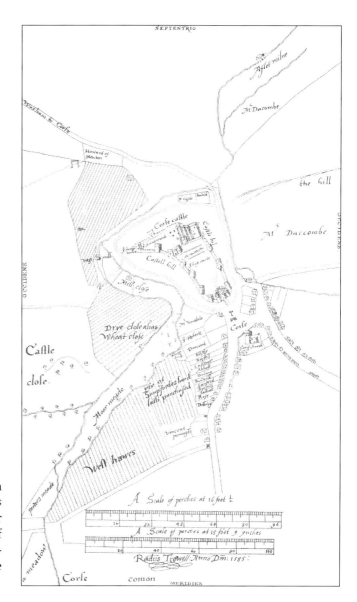

Two plans of Corfe Castle, which appeared originally in the first edition of John Hutchins' *History and Antiquities of the County of Dorset* in 1774, but were redrawn rather more clearly for the third edition. Both are the work of Ralph Treswell the elder of 1586. The Castle and its surrounding area at the top of this page (305 x 160) and the Castle alone at the bottom (195 x 255).

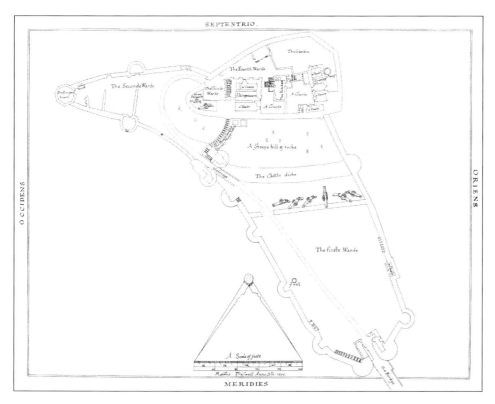

A south view of Corfe Castle by the brothers Samuel
and Nathaniel Buck, the famous eighteenth century
topographers. It is dated 1733 (145 x 355).

Two further engravings from the third edition of John Hutchins' *History and Antiquities of the County of Dorset*. Both views are anonymous and show Corfe Castle before and after demolition by mines and explosives due to its resistance to Parliament during the Civil War (before demolition 115 x 210 and after 105 x 210).

Above is a view of Corfe Castle in 1643 and below in 1660 after being reduced to a ruin. The artist is merely distinguished by the initials H.H.N.B. (both 85 x 142). Both drawings come from George Bankes' *History of Corfe Castle* of 1853.

Above is a view of Corfe Castle from the south west and below one from the south east. Both are engraved by J. H. Le Keux from his own drawings and are included in the third edition of John Hutchins' *History and Antiquities of the County of Dorset* (south-west view 150 x 310 and south-east view 170 x 275).

Two views of Corfe Castle from Thomas Bond's
History and Description of Corfe Castle of 1883. Above is a
drawing by Llewellynn Jewitt (90 x 170) and below one
produced by C. and E. Layton of London (100 x 195).

Above is a nearer view of Corfe Castle by Llewellynn Jewitt from Thomas Bond's *History and Description of Corfe Castle* (120 x 95) and below a sketch from a similar viewpoint by Charles G. Harper from his *Paddington to Penzance* of 1893 (95 x 130).

Two views of Corfe Castle by Joseph Pennell from Sir
Frederick Treves' *Highways and Byways in Dorset* of 1906
(above 65 x 90 and below 105 x 85).

Two views in the actual village of Corfe Castle, also by Joseph Pennell from Sir Frederick Treves' *Highways and Byways in Dorset* (above 100 x 80 and below 80 x 80).

Encombe House, 2½ miles south south west of Corfe Castle, is an important building of the eighteenth and early nineteenth century with alterations by Anthony Salvin from 1871 to 1874. Above is an engraving by V.M. Picot after a drawing by W. Tomkins from the first edition of John Hutchin's *History and Antiquities of the County of Dorset* of 1774 (200 x 395) and below an engraving by J.H. Le Keux after his own drawing from the third edition of the same work (155 x 305).

Above is an engraving of Lulworth Cove dated 1773 by the elder James Basire and also included in the first edition of John Hutchins' *History and Antiquities of the County of Dorset*. Below an engraving by George Cooke and etched by J.C. Allen of Lulworth Cliffs after a drawing by Samuel Prout from the *Southern Coast of England* of 1891 (80 x 110).

Two drawings of Lulworth Cove by Joseph Pennell
from Sir Frederick Treves' *Highways and Byways in
Dorset* of 1906 (above 65 x 85 and below 65 x 90).

Above is a view of old cottages at Ringstead Bay by Charles G. Harper from his *Dorset Coast* of 1905 (65 x 85) and below the arched rock called Durdle Door engraved by A. Birrell from a drawing by J. W. Upham dated 1 August 1804 in the *Beauties of England and Wales* (95 x 150). It is thought that J.M.W. Turner used Durdle Door as a model for the rock formation in his painting *Ulysses Deriding Polyphemus*.

Three views of Lulworth Castle, two from the first edition of John Hutchins' *History and Antiquities of the County of Dorset* of 1774 and the third from the third edition. Above is an anonymous view dated 1 August 1789 engraved by James Fittler from the third edition (290 x 400). Below left is a south-west view dated 1774 and engraved by the elder James Basire from a drawing by Giles Hulsey (215 x 355) and below right a north-east view dated 1773, also engraved by the elder James Basire from a drawing by J. Taylor (215 x 345). Lulworth Castle itself was built in about 1608 for Thomas Howard, 3rd Viscount Bindon and there were some eighteenth-century additions. The building was gutted by fire in 1929 and lay derelict for many years until partially restored and it is now in the care of English Heritage.

Two further views of Lulworth Castle. That above is by
J. P. Neale from Jones' *Views of the Seats of Noblemen and
Gentlemen* of 1829 (88 x 120) and below is a drawing by
Joseph Pennell from Sir Frederick Treves' *Highways and
Byways in Dorset* of 1906 (65 x 90).

WEYMOUTH

Weymouth owes its rise to prominence as a seaside town to the patronage of George III, who in 1789 was persuaded that sea bathing was good for general health and the strengthening of the constitution. He made regular visits to the town from that date until 1805 and his influence really put the town on the map. When he first took the momentous step of a dip in the briny, a small band concealed in a nearby bathing machine struck up 'God Save the King', something that was obviously a sensible precaution by enlisting the aid of the Almighty in such a hazardous venture. The good citizens of the town showed their appreciation of their

sovereign's presence over the years, by commissioning a small statue on a rather large plinth, which still stands on the Esplanade.

Before the eighteenth century Weymouth suffered a great deal from the attention of pirates, especially those of the French variety and this rather miserable existence culminated in a rough time during the Civil War. The ruins of Sandsfoot Castle bear witness to attempts at fortification, which never seemed actually to offer much protection to the town. Like most south-coast resorts with a lurid past over the centuries, Weymouth is now a pleasant place which is spread out along a most attractive bay.

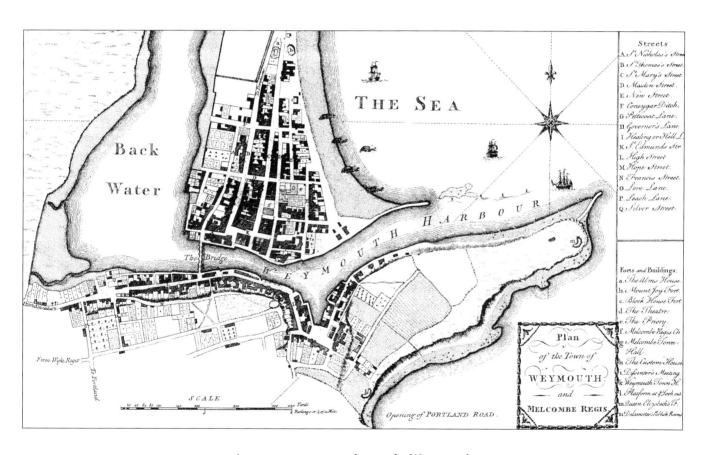

An anonymous plan of Weymouth engraved by somebody simply called Hall and included in the first edition of John Hutchins' *History and Antiquities of the County of Dorset* of 1774 (225 x 300).

Two Rock and Company engravings of Weymouth. Above is number 2942 dated 1 November 1855 (55 x 90) and below number 3103 dated 4 April 1856 showing Sandsfoot Castle with a distant view of the town (60 x 90). Rock and Company engravings were often sold in small booklets containing anything from half a dozen to a dozen views and pre-date similar collections of photographic views. Local printers and publishers all over the country were quick to copy the idea and many different varieties of these engravings can still be found.

Three views of Weymouth by Edmund H. Hew from Bertram Windle's *Wessex of Thomas Hardy* of 1902. Above is a re-working of an old drawing of George III's bathing machine (55 x 45) and in the centre more bathing machines on the beach (30 x 90) while below are sailing ships in the harbour (40 x 80).

Above is a view of Sandsfoot Castle with boats on or near the shoreline engraved by George Cooke from a drawing by Samuel Prout from the *Southern Coast of England* of 1891 (80 x 112) and below an engraving of the town from the third edition of *Jeffrey's Illustrated Guide to Weymouth* of 1856 (70 x 135).

Two views of the Weymouth shoreline with boats. Above is a drawing by Douglas Snowdon from Clive Holland's *Thomas Hardy's Wessex Scene* of 1948 (85 x 135) and below a sketch by Joseph Pennell from Sir Frederick Treves' *Highways and Byways in Dorset* of 1906 (65 x 90).

Above is a sketch of the front at Weymouth by Joseph Pennell from Sir Frederick Treves' *Highways and Byways in Dorset* of 1906 (45 x 90) and below a drawing by Charles G. Harper from his *Dorset Coast* of 1905, showing a cannon ball embedded at the top of the nearest wall, as a relic of the 1644 Civil War siege of the town (105 x 40).

Two further sketches of Weymouth by Joseph Pennell from Sir Frederick Treves' *Highways and Byways in Dorset*. The one above is of the harbour (125 x 90) and that below shows the bridge over the harbour (100 x 80).

A close-up view of buildings on the front at Weymouth by Edmund H. New from Bertram Windle's *Wessex of Thomas Hardy* of 1902 (142 x 90).

The mounted figure of George III cut in the chalk of the Downs near Osmington close to Weymouth. Above is a further sketch by Edmund H. New from Bertram Windle's *Wessex of Thomas Hardy* (80 x 90) and below a drawing by Joseph Pennell from Sir Frederick Treves' *Highways and Byways in Dorset* of 1906 (65 x 90).

Warmwell House is largely seventeenth-century in
construction with nineteenth-century additions. It has a
particularly complicated design and a striking internal
stone staircase. These two views are by Sidney Heath
from *Some Dorset Manor Houses* of 1907, written by him
in conjunction with W. de C. Prideaux (above 85 x 145
and below 165 x 230).

PORTLAND AND THE CHESIL BEACH

Portland is almost an island and only joined to the mainland by a slender causeway. It has always been a place apart, suspicious of outsiders known as 'kimberlins' and carried on life in its own ways. The area can be bleak and treeless with some sheep and what can only be called a little subsistence farming plus a small amount of fishing. However since Inigo Jones discovered the building potential of the local limestone, Portland has been making a very reasonable living by exporting itself to the rest of the country. Quarries now make up the bulk of the district, but there is also a ruined medieval castle, thought to have been created on the orders of William Rufus and now known as Bow and Arrow Castle. In addition there is one of Henry VIII's coastal defence fortresses, now in the care of English Heritage and a castellated country house designed by James Wyatt in 1800 and called Pennsylvania Castle. One unlovely blot on the landscape is a large prison and another a Borstal. There are a number of Victorian churches and two lighthouses.

The Chesil Beach runs from Portland to Burton Bradstock. It is a bank of pebbles graded by size with the biggest near Portland. It is said that local fishermen and smugglers in mist or at night could tell exactly where they were by the size of these pebbles. The whole area from West Bay along Chesil Beach had a fearsome reputation in the eighteenth and nineteenth centuries for shipwrecks and the churchyard at Wyke between Weymouth and Portland harbour contains the remains of numerous bodies washed up at that time.

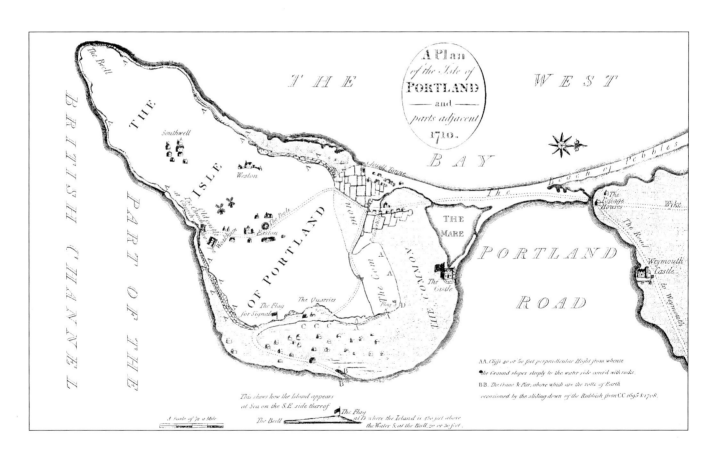

An anonymous plan of Portland dated 1710. It comes from the third edition of John Hutchins' *History and Antiquities of the County of Dorset* (210 x 360).

Two views of Portland. Above is an engraving by somebody simply called Bonner from *Jeffrey's Illustrated
Weymouth Guide* of 1856 showing a very crowded
harbour (50 x 75) and below Portland from Wyke
church, a sketch by Charles G. Harper from his *Dorset
Coast* of 1905 (95 x 165).

Two further views of Portland. Both are published by J. Sheeren of Weymouth and are undated. That above is entitled *Portland and the Breakwater* and the one below *Portland with the Breakwater* (above 65 x 105 and below 60 x 90).

An anonymous drawing of the Outer Gate of Portland Castle, Henry VIII's coastal defence fortress, which is now in the care of English Heritage. It comes from Charles Oman's *Castles* of 1926 (110 x 75).

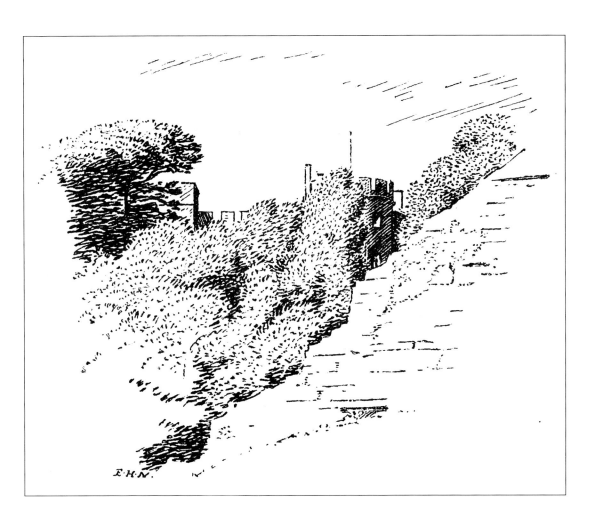

Pennsylvania Castle was designed in 1800 by James Wyatt for John Penn, the Governor of Portland, but in the fulness of time became an hôtel. The view above is by Edmund H. New from Bertram Windle's *Wessex of Thomas Hardy* of 1902 (70 x 85) and the drawing below is by Joseph Pennell from Sir Frederick Treves' *Highways and Byways in Dorset* of 1906 (65 x 90).

The original name for Bow and Arrow Castle in Portland was Rufus Castle, as it was believed to have been constructed by William Rufus. The first mention of the building is 1142 and most of it has now fallen down the cliff. Above is an engraving dated 1 April 1803 by William Woolnoth after a drawing by J.C. Smith from the *Beauties of England and Wales* (100 x 160) and below a sketch by Joseph Pennell from Sir Frederick Treves' *Highways and Byways in Dorset* of 1906 (60 x 75).

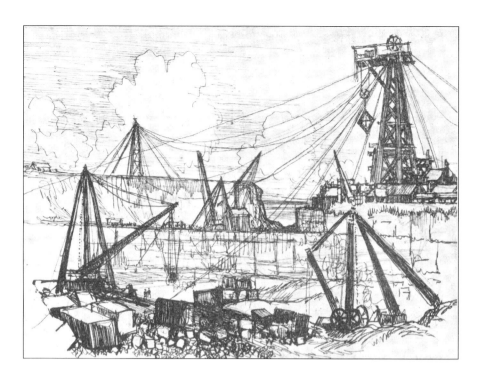

Two further drawings of Portland by Joseph Pennell from Sir Frederick Treves' *Highways and Byways in Dorset*. Above is a view of the stone quarries (65 x 90) and below Church Hope Cove (68 x 90).

Two anonymous views of Abbotsbury from the third edition of John Hutchins' *History and Antiquities of the County of Dorset*. Above is the malthouse (100 x 180) and below a view of St Catherine's chapel (85 x 165). The abbey was Benedictine and little remains of the original extensive eleventh-century monastic complex, but a fourteenth-century barn survives.

Two further views of St Catherine's chapel at Abbotsbury. This lovely building is partially Perpendicular and most unexpectedly has inside a stone tunnel vault. Above is an engraving by John Greig from a drawing by Edward Dayes included in the *Beauties of England and Wales* and dated 1803 (100 x 150) and below a sketch by Charles G. Harper from his *Dorset Coast* of 1905 (90 x 135).

The monastic buildings at Abbotsbury as they then existed nearly two centuries ago. Both views are by Edward Dayes, who died in 1804 and come from the *Antiquarian and Topographical Cabinet* of 1819. That above is engraved by James Storer and the one below by John Greig (both 60 x 85).

The abbey barn at Abbotsbury is one of the largest in England and seems to date from the fourteenth century with a seventeenth-century timber roof. Above is the porch sketched by Douglas Snowdon for Clive Holland's *Thomas Hardy's Wessex Scene* of 1948 (120 x 85) and below a drawing by Joseph Pennell from Sir Frederick Treves' *Highways and Byways in Dorset* of 1906 with St Catherine's chapel in the distance (65 x 90).

Above are some old cottages at Chesil and below the wreck of the Norwegian barque *Patria* on the Chesil Beach on 26 October 1903. Both views are by Charles G. Harper and come from his *Dorset Coast* of 1905 (above 55 x 95 and below 80 x 125).

BRIDPORT

Bridport is a small rather unpretentious town with wide and well proportioned streets, which is not so much a port as the giving out of the surrounding countryside into a foreshore. In the eighteenth century Defoe observed that there was a fair amount of fishing and the local magistrates placed a guard on the landing of catches, so that the country folk would not buy up quantities of fish to use as manure, a practice that was thought at the time to cause infection.

Charles II, disguised as a groom, passed briefly through the town after the Battle of Worcester, and although it was swarming with Parliamentary troops managed to make good his escape. In the eighteenth and nineteenth centuries the position of Bridport almost exactly between to the great naval bases of Portsmouth and Plymouth encouraged the growth of a thriving cordage industry. So important did this enterprise become for the town that some streets were laid out to facilitate the twining of the cord and to make rigging and all the hundred and one other articles used on ships of the period. The small late-eighteenth-century Town Hall with its cupola and clock is perhaps the building which best sums up the quiet and civilised good manners of the whole place.

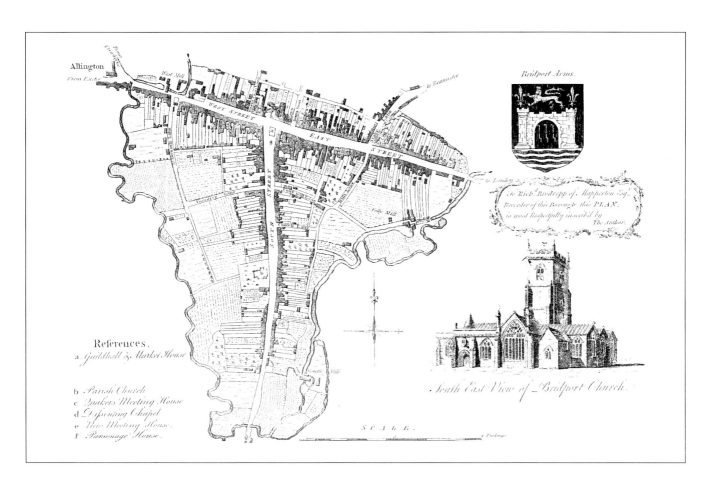

A plan of Bridport that also contains a south-east view of the church of St Mary, which has Early English transepts with most of the rest of the building being Perpendicular and finally some Victorian additions. The engraver is the elder James Basire after a drawing by B. Pryce and the work comes from the first edition of John Hutchins' *History and Antiquities of the County of Dorset* of 1774 (whole Plan 235 x 340 and St Mary's 80 x 120).

Above is a distant view of Bridport as seen by J.M.W. Turner in an engraving based on the painting from the *Southern Coast of England* series, the original of which is in the Bury Art Gallery. It is reproduced in F.J.H. Darton's *Marches of Wessex* of 1936 (95 x 120). Below is a drawing of West Bay, Bridport by Joseph Pennell from Sir Frederick Treves' *Highways and Byways in Dorset* of 1906 (60 x 90).

Above is a further view of West Bay. It is by Douglas Snowdon from Clive Holland's *Thomas Hardy's Wessex Scene* of 1948 (95 x 85) and below is a sketch of the Town Hall in Bridport by Joseph Pennell from Sir Frederick Treves' *Highways and Byways in Dorset* (70 x 90).

Bridport Town Hall and the facade of the Ship Inn by
Edmund H. New from Bertram Windle's *Wessex of
Thomas Hardy* of 1902 (142 x 90).

Two views of the building that was once the Castle Inn in Bridport. Above is a drawing by Charles G. Harper from his *Dorset Coast* of 1905 (85 x 95) and below a sketch by Herbert Railton from W. Outram Tristram's *Coaching Days and Coaching Ways* of 1893 (60 x 65).

The Packhorse Inn in Bridport as seen by Herbert Railton in 1893. The sketch is included in W. Outram Tristram's *Coaching Days and Coaching Ways* of that date (125 x 90).

Above is a north-east view of Chideock Castle. It shows the remnants of a once large and impressive gatehouse of a building probably constructed in the 1430s. Now all that remains are a few ditches. The illustration comes from the third edition of John Hutchins' *History and Antiquities of the County of Dorset* (70 x 135). Below is a sketch of the village of Chideock by Joseph Pennell from Sir Frederick Treves' *Highways and Byways in Dorset* of 1906 (50 x 90).

Two further views of Chideock. Above is a drawing by Charles G. Harper from his *Exeter Road* of 1899 (55 x 90) and below a sketch by J.W. King from *Where Dorset Meets Devon* of 1914 by Francis Bickley (60 x 100).

Two illustrations from the third edition of John Hutchins' *History and Antiquities of the County of Dorset*. Above is a view of the church of St Mary, Netherbury, which has a high Perpendicular tower with a largely Decorated interior and some Victorian work. The engraving is by B. Howlett after a drawing by John Buckler (110 x 165). Below is an engraving of the Hyde near Bridport by J.H. Le Keux after his own drawing (135 x 275).

The tower of the church of St Candida, Whitchurch Canonicorum, a building with a small amount of Norman work, but predominantly of Early English and Perpendicular construction with some Victorian restoration. The tower itself is Perpendicular and this illustration by J.W. King comes from Francis Bickley's *Where Dorset Meets Devon* of 1914 (130 x 85).

Two views of the village of Whitchurch Canonicorum.
Above is a drawing by Joseph Pennell from Sir
Frederick Treves' *Highways and Byways in Dorset* of 1906
(65 x 90) and below a sketch by J.W. King from Francis
Bickley's *Where Dorset Meets Devon* (65 x 100).

CHARMOUTH AND LYME REGIS

Lyme Regis received a royal borough charter as early as Edward I's reign and owes its existence as a harbour to the Cobb, an artificially created pier. Its early history saw numerous raids by the French and prosperity arising from fishing, smuggling and trade with the West Indies, Newfoundland and the near Continent. The town clusters on a steep hillside and resisted a siege by Royalists in the Civil War. Defoe found it an extremely pleasant place to visit and it became famous as the port where the Duke of Monmouth landed while making his ill-fated attempt on the English throne. By the eighteenth century it had in essence become a small watering place and achieved a comfortable existence by the time of Jane Austen's visit in 1804, something that continued in spite of an extensive fire in 1844.

Charmouth is slightly to the east of Lyme Regis and its chief moment in the limelight of history was when the Danes descended on the Saxons in two bloody raids in the 830s. After the Battle of Worcester Charles II was in Charmouth briefly while trying to charter a ship to take him into exile. Since that date nothing of national moment has overtaken this small coastal town.

Two views of Charmouth by J.W. King from Francis Brickley's *Where Dorset Meets Devon* of 1914. Above is the beach (52 x 100) and below Church Cliff with some houses (70 x 100).

Above is further sketch in Charmouth by J.W. King from Francis Brickley's *Where Dorset Meets Devon* (95 x 120) and below a view over Lyme Regis by John Drayton Junior of 1840 reproduced in C. Wanklyn's *Lyme Regis* of 1927 (95 x 165).

Rock and Company engravings numbers 2425 and 2426, both dated 1 May 1854. Above is a view of Lyme Regis from Holme Bush and below one from Charmouth (both 60 x 95).

Above is Rock and Company's engraving No. 1842 dated 20 July 1855. It shows the beach at Lyme Regis where the Duke of Monmouth landed to start his ill-fated attempt on the crown (60 x 95) and below a view of the devastating fire in the town on 11 May 1844. It comes from the *Illustrated London News* of 18 May 1844 (60 x 75).

Two views of the Cobb at Lyme Regis by J.W. King from
Francis Bickley's *Where Dorset Meets Devon* of 1914
(above 70 x 110 and below 70 x 160).

Two views of the front at Lyme Regis by Joseph Pennell.
Above is a drawing for Sir Frederick Treves' *Highways
and Byways in Dorset* of 1906 and below a sketch from
Arthur Norway's *Highways and Byways in Devon and
Cornwall* of 1897 (above 60 x 90 and below 85 x 140).

Above is a sketch of a corner of the Parade
at Lyme Regis by J.W. King from Francis
Bickley's *Where Dorset Meets Devon* of 1914
(70 x 105) and below the River Buddle in
the town by Joseph Pennell from Sir
Francis Treves' *Highways and Byways in
Dorset* of 1906 (112 x 85).

Two further drawings in Lyme Regis by J.W. King from *Where Dorset Meets Devon*. Above is a view of St Michael's church (90 x 75) and below Coombe Court with a picturesque alleyway (95 x 65).

COOMBE
COURT.

BEAMINSTER

eaminster is a cheerful little country town nestling in a hollow between hills with architecture of the nineteenth century and later. This character came about because like several other notable places in the county it suffered a number of extensive fires. The first of these occurred in the Civil War by something as trivial as the accidental discharge of a musket into the thatch of a house. Trivial or not, it succeeded in burning down most of the town and similar destruction followed in both 1684 and 1781. However, the parish church of St Mary luckily survives and has one of the most glorious towers in the county, which is the equal of many of the famous Somerset towers.

Above is a view of Beaminster 'sketched from nature and lithographed by W. Spreat, Exeter' from George Pulman's *Book of the Axe* of 1875 (116 x 193) and below the carving on Beaminster church tower by William Curtis Green from the *Builder* of 20 August 1904. As a legacy was made in 1503 for the building of the tower, this gives its approximate date (160 x 155).

Above is a drawing of the modest almshouses beside the churchyard in Beaminster, a gift of Sir John Strode of Parnham in 1630. The drawing by Sidney Heath comes from his *Old English Houses of Alms* of 1910 (110 x 155). Below is a sketch by Joseph Pennell from Sir Frederick Treves' *Highways and Byways in Dorset* of 1906. It is of Mapperton House near Beaminster, a happy blend of seventeenth-century work with that of the following two centuries in warm Ham Hill stone (65 x 90).

Two views by Sidney Heath from *Some Dorset Manor Houses*, written by himself and W. de C. Prideaux in 1907. They are of Parnham house just outside Beaminster. The house is originally of the mid-sixteenth century with enlargements in the seventeenth and early-nineteenth centuries and restorations and alterations in the early-twentieth century (above 85 x 150 and below 165 x 212).

Hiding Place. Exterior.

Hiding Place. Interior.

Trent Manor House
Sidney Heath.

Trent Manor House near Sherborne is fifteenth century with seventeenth century alterations and further work at the beginning of the eighteenth century. The drawings are also by Sidney Heath from *Some Dorset Manor Houses* (whole plate 215 x 165).

FORDE ABBEY

Although much altered Forde Abbey must be accounted a miraculous survival and is surrounded by one of the most important gardens in England. The story begins when it was founded by the Cistercians in 1141 and twelfth- and thirteenth-century work is incorporated in the present building. At the time of the Dissolution it became the property of Henry Pollard and in 1649 was bought by Edmund Prideaux, Attorney General under Cromwell. It thus escaped destruction in the Civil War and both Pollard and Prideaux by adding considerably to the structure, succeeded in creating a house of very high quality.

Above is a lithograph by W. Spreat after his own drawing included in George Pulman's *Book of the Axe* of 1875 (107 x 187) and below a drawing by Herbert Railton from W. Outram Tristram's *Coaching Days and Coaching Ways* of 1893 (63 x 90). Both views emphasise the happy grouping of the various parts of Forde Abbey.

Two views of detailed parts of Forde Abbey by J.W. King from Francis Bickley's *Where Dorset Meets Devon* of 1914 (above 70 x 100 and below 75 x 100).

SHERBORNE

For some three-hundred-and-seventy years from 705 to 1075 Sherborne was the seat of a bishop before the see was removed to Old Sarum and then the present cathedral of Salisbury. From 998 the former cathedral in Sherborne became monastic, a situation which prevailed until the Dissolution, when the abbey church was sold to the town and has remained the parish church ever since. Parts of the abbey buildings were incorporated into Sherborne School with Victorian restorations and additions by R.C. and R.H. Carpenter and Sir Reginald Blomfield.

The town still retains almshouses built some five-hundred-and-fifty years ago and the ruins of a once mighty castle, which was beseiged in the Civil War until taken by Fairfax for Parliament and subsequently slighted. Thereafter Sherborne Lodge, built by Sir Walter Raleigh, became known as Sherborne Castle, the seat of the Digbys. One unique feature of the town is the monks' conduit that was built in the sixteenth century and stood originally in the monastic cloister. It has now been re-sited in the area by the east gateway to the abbey precinct. Taken altogether the town is one of the most attractive in the county.

A south view of Sherborne Abbey, which appeared originally in Sir William Dugdale's *Monasticon Anglicanum* published between 1655 and 1673. The artist is Richard Newcourt and the engraver Daniel King, who is thought to have died in 1664. The latter published a series of the engravings from the *Monasticon* in 1656 under the title *Cathedrall and Conventuall Churches of England and Wales*. King's engravings are fairly basic, but nevertheless give an impression of the abbey in the seventeenth century. Dugdale had a low opinion of King and described him as 'an ignorant silly fellow ... an arrant knave' (170 x 295).

Above is an engraving of Sherborne Abbey dated 1803 by J. Smith from a drawing by John Buckler included in the *Beauties of England and Wales* (100 x 150) and below a further engraving by Daniel King of the abbey from an anonymous drawing in *Cathedrall and Conventuall Churches* (240 x 170).

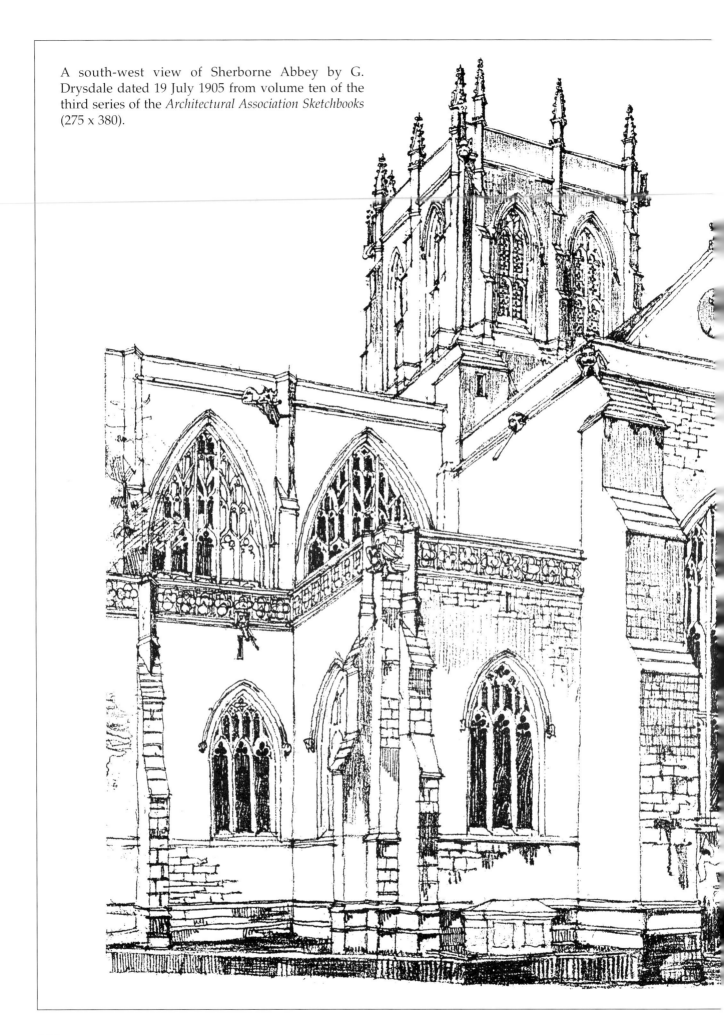

A south-west view of Sherborne Abbey by G. Drysdale dated 19 July 1905 from volume ten of the third series of the *Architectural Association Sketchbooks* (275 x 380).

Two almost exactly similar views of Sherborne Abbey. Above is an engraving of 1803 by T.L. Busby from a drawing by F.W.L. Stockdale after a sketch by George Shepherd from the *Beauties of England and Wales* (100 x 150) and below an engraving by John Greig or James Storer after a drawing by Edward Dayes from the *Antiquarian and Topographical Cabinet* of 1819. However as Dayes died in 1804 and the two views are so similar and must have been made almost at the same time, it would be interesting to know if either artist was aware of the other's work (70 x 100).

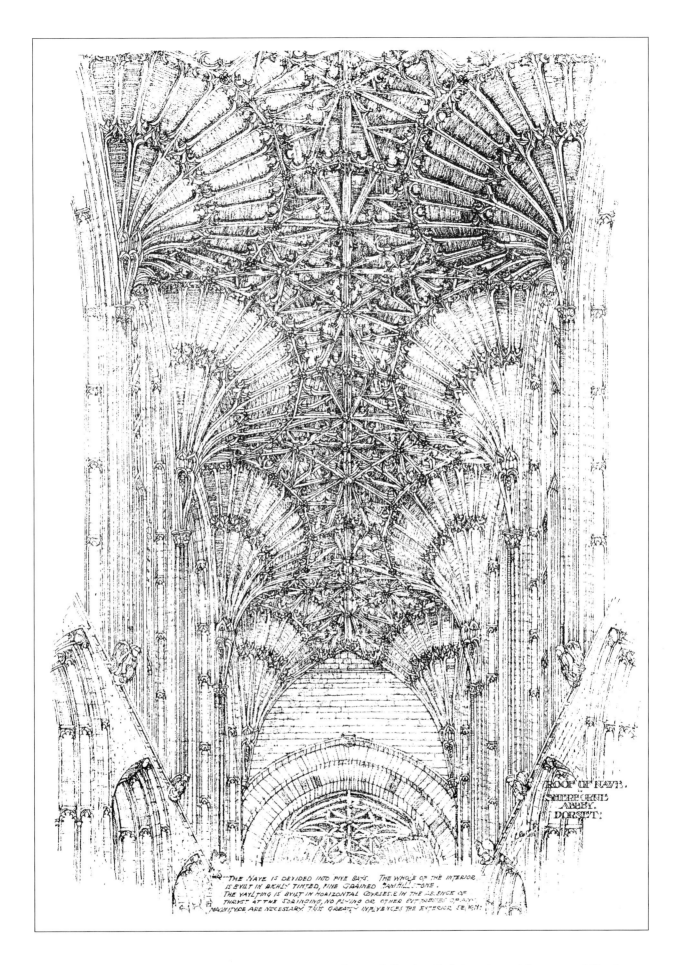

A beautifully detailed drawing of the nave of Sherborne
Abbey made in 1905 by E. Garrat, which appears in the
Architectural Association Sketchbook of 1909 (380 x 275).

Above is a drawing of the monks' conduit and abbey tower in Sherborne by Joseph Pennell from Sir Frederick Treves' *Highways and Byways in Dorset* of 1906 (60 x 90) and below two detailed drawings of the conduit alone by G. Drysdale made in August 1905 and included in volume ten of the third series of the *Architectural Association Sketchbooks*. The conduit was built by Abbot Mere in the early sixteenth century as the lavatorium for the monks in the abbey cloister. It now stands near the east gateway of the abbey precinct (155 x 280).

Above is Joseph Pennell's drawing from Sir Frederick Treves' *Highways and Byways in Dorset* of the west window and south porch of Sherborne Abbey (60 x 90). Below is an engraving of Sherborne Castle (formerly Lodge) drawn by John Buckler and engraved by George Cooke, from the third edition of Hutchins' *History and Antiquities of the County of Dorset*, (197 x 325).

Hospital of S.S.John
Sherborne Dorset

Sidney Heath

The almshouses of St John the Baptist and St John the Evangelist in Trendle Street, Sherborne. The original building of 1437 and 1438 was for twelve poor men and four poor women with dormitory accommodation for the men below and the women above them. In 1858 an expansion allowed separate rooms for the inmates and there is also a chapel and refectory with an open-ended arcaded cloister. Above is a drawing by Sidney Heath from his *Old English Houses of Alms* of 1910 (195 x 165) and below a sketch by Joseph Pennell showing the cloister and chapel from Sir Frederick Treves *Highways and Byways in Dorset* of 1906 (60 x 90).

Above is a view of St Augustine's Hospital in Sherborne as it appeared in 1803. The engraving is by W. and G. Cooke after a drawing by John Buckler from the *Beauties of England and Wales* (90 x 145) and below a sketch of the remains of the old, once mighty castle, built by Bishop Roger of Salisbury between 1107 and 1135 and slighted after the Civil War. The artist is Joseph Pennell and the sketch also comes from *Highways and Byways in Dorset* (55 x 90).

All that remains of the once proud Benedictine Abbey of Cerne, founded originally in the late ninth century, are the entrance gateway, the porch to the abbot's hall, the so-called guest house and a barn, all now part of a farm. Above is an engraving of the entrance gateway dated 2 May 1803. It is by J. Smith from a drawing by J.W. Upham in the *Beauties of England and Wales* (145 x 93). Below is the same view with an artist hard at work drawn by J.J. Hissey from his book *On Southern English Roads* of 1896 (163 x 100).

Two more views of the remains of the Cerne Abbey gateway. Above is a drawing by Joseph Pennell from Sir Frederick Treves' *Highways and Byways in Dorset* of 1906 (115 x 90) and below an engraving of 1819 by James Storer after a drawing by Edward Dayes in the *Antiquarian and Topographical Cabinet*. As Dayes died in 1804 the drawing was obviously made some time before the engraving was produced for the publication (85 x 55).

Bingham's Melcombe midway between Blandford and Dorchester is a manor house of the sixteenth and seventeenth centuries with other work at the end of the nineteenth century. The two views are by Sidney Heath from *Some Dorset Manor Houses* of 1907, written by him and W. de C. Prideaux. See also pages 175 and 176. (above 80 x 145 and below 212 x 170.)

Two drawings of Bingham's Melcombe by Joseph Pennell from Sir Frederick Treves' *Highways and Byways in Dorset* of 1906. Above is the courtyard and below is the bowling green, part of the very interesting gardens restored by G.A. Jellicoe in the twentieth century. (above 65 x 95 and below 65 x 90).

Chantmarle

Chantmarle is a manor house roughly in the middle of an imaginary triangle drawn between Sherborne, Bridport and Dorchester. It was built during the first quarter of the seventeenth century and has twentieth century additions. This view by Sidney Heath comes from *Some Dorset Manor Houses* written by him conjunction with W. de C. Prideaux (195 x 180).

DORCHESTER

Dorchester is the county town and on busy shopping days the long High Street has a strongly urban feel about it. In the centre of this thoroughfare is situated St Peter's the mother church of the town, which is largely Perpendicular in construction and mercifully escaped destruction in a major conflagration in 1613 and various other smaller fires in 1622, 1725 and 1775. It is therefore not surprising that the feel of the town from the past is largely late eighteenth and nineteenth century.

In the Civil War the town came out strongly for Parliament and although surrendered initially without a shot to the Royalists it changed hands several times before it was seized again for Parliament by Lord Essex. Dorchester gained notoriety more than a century later when the Bloody Assize was initiated by Judge Jeffreys after the Duke of Monmouth's futile rebellion. Many of the accused faced very flimsy charges, but notwithstanding the lack of real evidence 80% were either executed or transported.

Close to the town is Maiden Castle, one of the most stupendous prehistoric sites in Britain and there are also a number of attractive country houses in the near vicinity.

An undated plan of Dorchester engraved by Bayly after a drawing by B. Pryce from John Hutchins' *History and Antiquities of the County of Dorset* of 1774 (315 x 235).

Two distant views of Dorchester. Above is a drawing made by an artist in the entourage of Cosmo III, Grand Duke of Tuscany, who on making a visit to the south of England in 1669 was received as an honoured guest in the houses of the nobility and gentry. The Duke's travels were issued as a publication in this country by J. Mawman in 1821 when Thomas Hosmer Shepherd was engaged to re-work the original drawings in sepia aquatinting, one of his strangest commissions (150 x 260). Below is an undated sketch by an artist distinguished only be the initials A.B. from the *Southern and Western Coast* volume of the *Rivers of Britain* of 1897 (145 x 205).

Two sketches of the centre of Dorchester by Edmund H. New from Bertram Windle's *Wessex of Thomas Hardy* of 1902. Above is a view of the London Road and below near St Peter's (both 142 x 90).

Two further views in Dorchester. Above is a sketch by Charles G. Harper from the *Exeter Road* of 1899 (105 x 145) and below where Judge Jeffries lodged. The drawing is by Herbert Railton in W. Outram Tristram's *Coaching Days and Coaching Ways* of 1893 (100 x 90).

Above is another sketch by Edmund H. New of the so-called Hangman's Cottage in Dorchester, also from Bertram Windle's *Wessex of Thomas Hardy* (90 x 75) and a further drawing by Herbert Railton from *Coaching Days and Coaching Ways*, this time of the White Hart in Dorchester (85 x 90).

Thomas Hardy is almost certainly Dorset's most famous literary son and above is his seated statue in Dorchester. The drawing is by Douglas Snowdon from Clive Holland's Thomas Hardy's *Wessex Scene* of 1948 (130 x 90). Below is a sketch of Napper's Mite almshouses, founded by Sir Robert Napper in 1616 with a street front of 1842. They are situated in South Street, Dorchester, and the view is by Sidney Heath from his *Old English Houses of Alms* of 1910 (210 x 168).

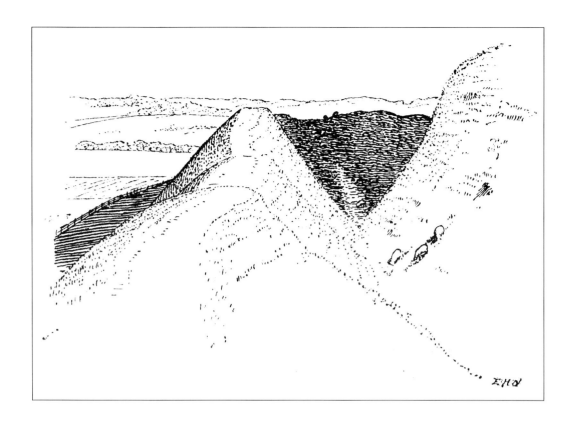

Maiden Castle is a mighty series of earthworks just outside Dorchester. Above is a sketch of them by Edmund H. New from Bertram Windle's *Wessex of Thomas Hardy* of 1902 (65 x 90) and below one of Thomas Hosmer Shepherd's sepia aquatints after an unknown artist in the entourage of Cosmo III, Grand Duke of Tuscany (see page 162). The original artist made the earthworks look like a series of pieces of layered cake and the whole view seems to be a product of imagination rather than observation (150 x 255).

Athelhampton near Dorchester has a late Perpendicular hall and mid-sixteenth century parlour wing and the whole ensemble has had considerable modifications since its original construction. The drawings are both by Joseph Nash from his *Mansions of England in the Olden Time* of 1838 to 1849, in which he recreates furniture, fittings and people's dress relevant to the original date of a building. The view above shows the courtyard with a couple of young bucks squaring off to each other, while the one below features a game of blind man's buff (both 140 x 190).

Waterson or Waterston Manor is also near Dorchester and a delight-
ful seventeenth-century building. There was reconstruction in 1864
after a fire the previous year and remodelling in 1911. This view is
another by Joseph Nash from his *Mansions of England in the Olden
Time* (205 x 145).

Cranborne Manor House started life as a royal hunting lodge in Cranborne Chase, being rebuilt by King John from 1207 to 1208. This original lodge was incorporated into a new house in the reign of James I and the west wing altered in 1647, with the east wing being demolished in 1712. The interiors however are largely nineteenth century. The two drawings are by Joseph Pennell from Sir Frederick Treves' *Highways and Byways in Dorset* of 1906 (above 65 x 90 and below 110 x 80).

Poxwell Manor House

The Gatehouse

Poxwell Manor is south east of Dorchester and dates
from the first half of the seventeenth century. The view
is by Sidney Heath from this *Some Dorset Manor Houses*
of 1907, written in conjunction with W. de C. Prideaux
(215 x 180).

South East

Woodsford Castle

West End

N.E. Tower and Dungeon

Newel Stair

Woodsford Castle almost due east of Dorchester dates from the fourteenth century and a licence to crenellate was granted in 1335. There were originally four corner towers and a fifth on the long east wall and now only the north-eastern one survives. The drawing is by Sidney Heath from his *Some Dorset Manor Houses* written in 1907 in conjunction with W. de C. Prideaux (whole Plate 210 x 170).

Wolfeton

Arms on Gatehouse

The Gatehouse

Another of Sidney Heath's drawings from *Some Dorset Manor Houses*. It is of Wolfeton House just north of Dorchester. The house was built early in the sixteenth century and enlarged some fifty years later. However, only the gatehouse and the south-west corner of the main building survive, as the remaining parts were demolished in the early-eighteenth century (Whole Plate 195 x 175).

Winterbourne Anderson

Anderson Manor is situated between Wimborne and Dorchester. It dates from 1622 and externally has hardly been altered, but internally almost completely changed. The drawing is another by Sidney Heath from his *Some Dorset Manor Houses* written in 1907 in conjunction with W. de. C. Prideaux (Whole Plate 225 x 165).

ACKNOWLEDGEMENTS

A work of this kind cannot be compiled without the advice and help of a large number of people and I would like to acknowledge with grateful thanks assistance from the following institutions and people: the Society of Antiquaries for permission to reproduce material and especially Bernard Nurse, the Librarian, and his ever courteous staff; the always help-ful staff of the London Library; my wife Marion for her expert advice as an architectural historian; Steven Pugsley and his staff at Dorset Books for steering me down the rapids of compilation; but finally and not least, an especial vote of thanks to the memory of all those artists and engravers whose skills illumine the past here in such fascinating detail.

The inner courtyard of Bingham's Melcombe House (see also page 158). This view is one by Joseph Nash from his *Mansions of England in the Olden Times* of 1838-1849 in which the people are wear-ing clothes appropriate to the time at which the house was originally built (205 x 145).

SUGGESTIONS FOR FURTHER READING

I have mentioned a large number of books and periodicals in the main body of the text and captions and it is pointless to repeat them here. Readers will obviously make their own judgements about whether they wish to consult them further and in any event, they vary considerably in value, accuracy and usefulness.

For biographical information in general the *Dictionary of National Biography* and *Who Was Who* are essential. More specialist works I have found useful are Simon Houfe's *Dictionary of Nineteenth Century British Book Illustrators* (revised edition 1996) and Ronald Russell's *Guide to Topographical Prints* (1979), but above all Bernard Adams' *London Illustrated 1604-1851* (1983). This outstanding work of scholarship deals not only with exclusively London material, but also publications covering the whole country that have London sections, and therefore includes a mass of useful detail about artists and engravers found in the present volume. The equally outstanding *Dictionary of British Architects 1600-1840* by Sir Howard Colvin (revised edition 1993) is indispensable and the *Dictionary of British Architects 1834-1914* (new edition 2001) brings the story up to the early-twentieth century. The Dorset volume of the *Buildings of England* series by John Newman and Sir Nikolaus Pevsner (1972) is still relevant but needs revising, while the Royal Commission on Historical Monuments volumes on the county range from 1952 to the 1970s. However the *Victoria County History of Dorset* has hardly got off the ground as volume two was published in 1908 and volume three not until sixty years later.

Books of a more general nature published before the Second World War have a period charm, but of course can no longer be read for current information. They include Frank Heath's *Dorset* in the Little Guides series (1905), Alfred Pope's *Old Stone Crosses of Dorset* (1906), Thomas Perkins and Herbert Pentin's *Memorials of Old Dorset* (1907), Donald Maxwell's *Unknown Dorset* (1927),

J.H. Wade's *Rambles in Dorset* (1931), H.O. Locke's *Dorset* (1934), Llewellyn Powys' *Dorset Essays* (1935), Geoffrey Clark and W. Harding Thompson's *Dorset* in the County landscapes series (1935), the *Shell Guide to Dorset* by Paul Nash with four of his own watercolours (1935), which were left out of the 1966 revision by Michael Pitt-Rivers and Dorothy Gardiner's *Companion into Dorset* (1937).

Works published after the Second World War naturally become more relevant to the present. In the 1950s they include Eric Benfield's *Dorset* in the Hale County series (1950), Margaret Goldworthy's *Dorset Bedside Anthology* with an introduction by the well-known farmer and broadcaster Ralph Wightman (1951), Marianne Dacombe's *Dorset Up Along Down Along* (1951), Olive Knott's *Down Dorset Way* (1954), a number of works by F.S. Hinchy among which are the *Heart of Dorset* (1952) and *North East Dorset Towns and Downs* (1957), Arthur Oswald's revised and enlarged edition of his *Country Houses of Dorset* (1959) and L.V. Grinsell's *Dorset Barrows* published by the Dorset Natural History and Archaeology Society (1959).

In the 1960s and 1970s are two more works by F.S. Hinchy *Dorset Days* (1960) and *Dorset Today and Yesterday* (1965), Ralph Wightman's own *Portrait of Dorset* (1965), Ronald Good's new edition of the *Old Roads of Dorset* (1966), Rachel Lloyd's *Dorset Elizabethans* (1967), Barbara Kerr's *Bound to the Soil - A Social History of Dorset* (1968), Christopher Taylor's *Dorset* in the Making of the English Landscape Series (1970), David Burnett's *Dorset Camera – Photographs 1855-1914* (1974) and Peter Irvine's *Victorian and Edwardian Dorset From Old Photographs* (1977).

From 1980 and beyond are Cecil Cullingford's *History of Dorset* (1980), Roland Grant's *Dorset Villages* (1980), David Cecil's *Some Dorset County Houses* (1985), Jo Draper's *Dorset – The Complete Guide* (1986) and Tim Goodwin's *Dorset in the Civil War 1625-1665* covering a particularly turbulent period in the county's history (1996).

The garden steps at Bingham's Melcombe (see also page 158). The drawing is by Sidney Heath from his *Some Dorset Manor Houses* of 1907 written in conjunction with W. de C. Prideaux (65 x 90).